I0390714

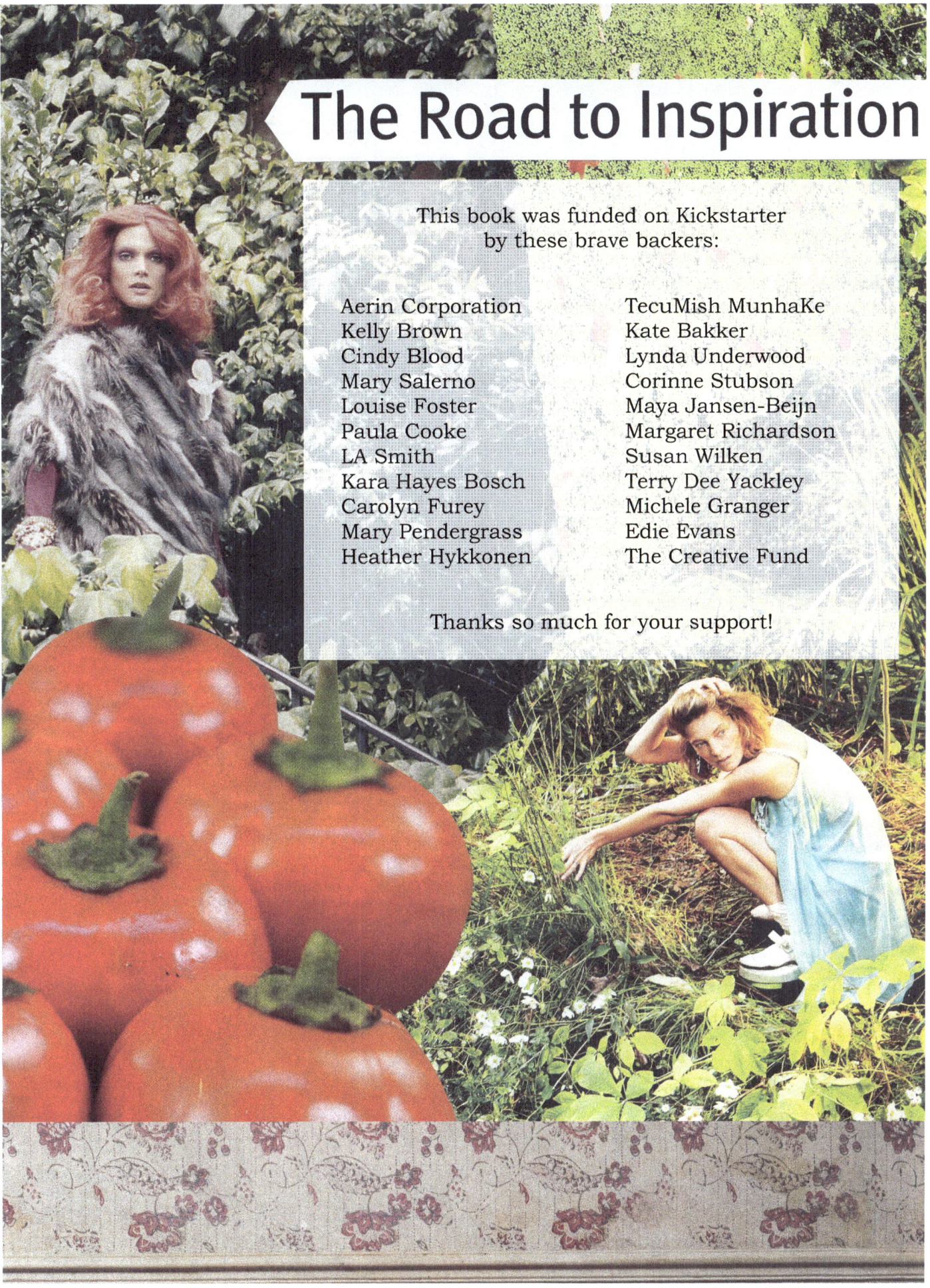

The Road to Inspiration

This book was funded on Kickstarter
by these brave backers:

Aerin Corporation
Kelly Brown
Cindy Blood
Mary Salerno
Louise Foster
Paula Cooke
LA Smith
Kara Hayes Bosch
Carolyn Furey
Mary Pendergrass
Heather Hykkonen

TecuMish MunhaKe
Kate Bakker
Lynda Underwood
Corinne Stubson
Maya Jansen-Beijn
Margaret Richardson
Susan Wilken
Terry Dee Yackley
Michele Granger
Edie Evans
The Creative Fund

Thanks so much for your support!

My Journey With Gluebooks

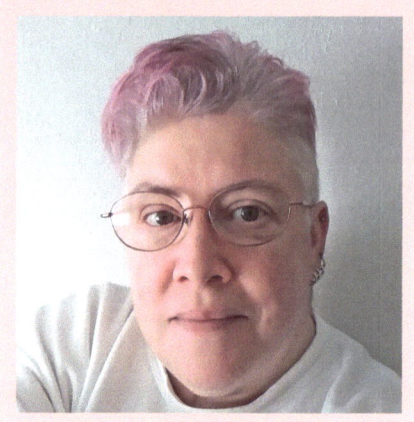

In 2004, I was making the transition from the corporate offices of the world's largest craft retailer to a small arts and crafts publishing company. My new job included keeping my eyes open for new ideas that could be developed into how-to books, and companies that could partner with us to help promote their products. Our design team was very creative, and could spin almost any idea or product into a book concept pretty quickly.

One Saturday, I was way down an internet rabbit hole, following links on artist sites to lead me places I might not see with a simple search. I clicked my way to a site that belonged to an artist in the Netherlands, with lots of photos, and not a lot of text. The one word that did jump out at me was *gluebook*. What the heck is a gluebook? I searched, and didn't find anything, so I flipped through the artist's site, looking for links to other people who might be doing the same thing, and found a few, but still no text.

Images told me a lot, and I made up the rest. I wrote a quick description of what I thought a gluebook was in the first English language article about them, *Discovering Gluebooks*, written for my web site, Go Make Something. The article was illustrated with my own first attempts at gluebooking. I also started an online group for people who wanted to give it a try.

On Monday morning, I brought the idea to my boss at the publishing company. I was fascinated with the whole idea of gluebooks, because they required no products or techniques at all. There was literally nobody at our company who could figure out a way to turn them into a how-to book idea. In a sea of technique heavy, product heavy creative outlets like scrapbooking, art journaling, and altered books, gluebooks stood alone. My boss shook her head at gluebooks, and moved on to the next idea.

I did not move on. For the next 15 years, I gluebooked. I hosted groups, changing platforms as social media took off. I've hosted endless numbers of gluecard swaps, and the Gluecard a Day project (GCAD). I've written articles about the joys of gluebooking.

And now, here's the book I couldn't figure how to write all those years ago. Whip out that glue stick...

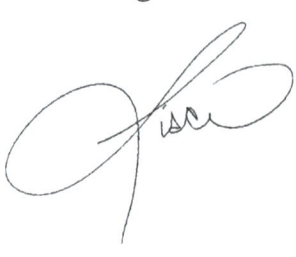

Lisa Vollrath is a prolific mixed-media artist, writer and designer. Her work covers a multitude of techniques, from altered books and collage, to textile art and costume design. She teaches classes and designs products for Ten Two Studios, the company she started in 2005.

Lisa has written dozens of books and how-to articles for arts and crafts publishers. Her current work can always been seen on her ever-growing web site, LisaVollrath.com.

fine products for mixed-media artists...

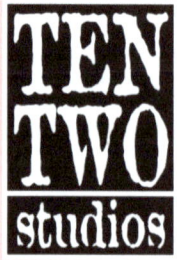

TEN TWO studios

Visit online at TenTwoStudios.com or email at TenTwoStudios@yahoo.com

What is a Gluebook?

A gluebook is a collage journal, generally created by gluing magazine images and other paper ephemera to pages. Unlike art journals, they do not rely on paints, rubber stamps, stickers, scrapbook papers, or other purchased craft products. Gluebooks put the emphasis on working with what you find, rather than purchasing what you need to create pages.

Gluebooks also do not require learning new, progressively difficult to achieve techniques. You cut. You glue. That's pretty much it.

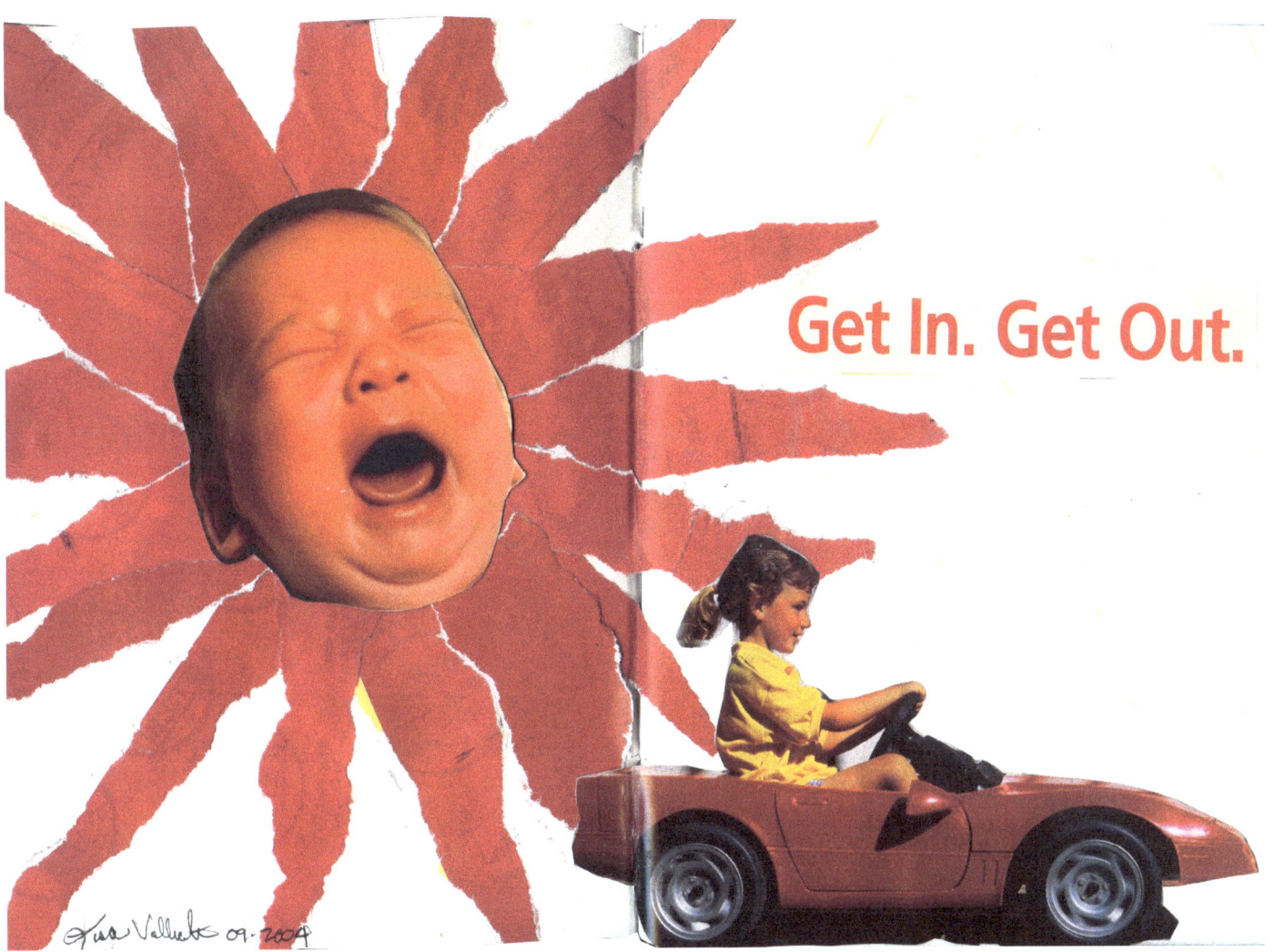

Get In. Get Out.

Although gluebooks don't use the same products or techniques as scrapbooks or art journals, they can certainly function as either of these things. Some gluebookers incorporate photos, receipts, concert tickets, bills, and other everyday paper fallout from their lives, creating a sort of scrapbook or visual journal of what's going on that day.

Why do people gluebook? Because it's an easy, fun way to create, that doesn't have the steep learning curve of other paper arts. Gluebooks provide a low stress way to figure out how to combine elements, and create interesting compositions. They're a great tool for honing your visual skills, without investing a lot of time and money. I use my gluebooks to clear my head, and just play between large, complex projects.

I've been moderating gluebook groups on various platforms since 2004. New gluebookers invariably ask the same questions:

What book should I use?

The simple answer to this is whatever book you want to use. I've seem people gluebook in all types of blank journals, old books, hand-made books, and composition books. There is no standard size, or shape, or number of pages.

A few tips, though:

Don't use a book with glossy pages until you're a little more experienced, because glossy magazine pages glued to glossy book pages often results in the images peeling off the page.

Start with something you can hold easily in your hand, with not a lot of pages. An old book for kids is perfect. Think of your first book as a test. You may find yourself saying, "I wish these pages were bigger" or "I wish these pages were heavier", and those thoughts will lead you to the right book next time.

Don't feel you have to fill a book before you start another one. I often have two or three gluebooks going, of different sizes.

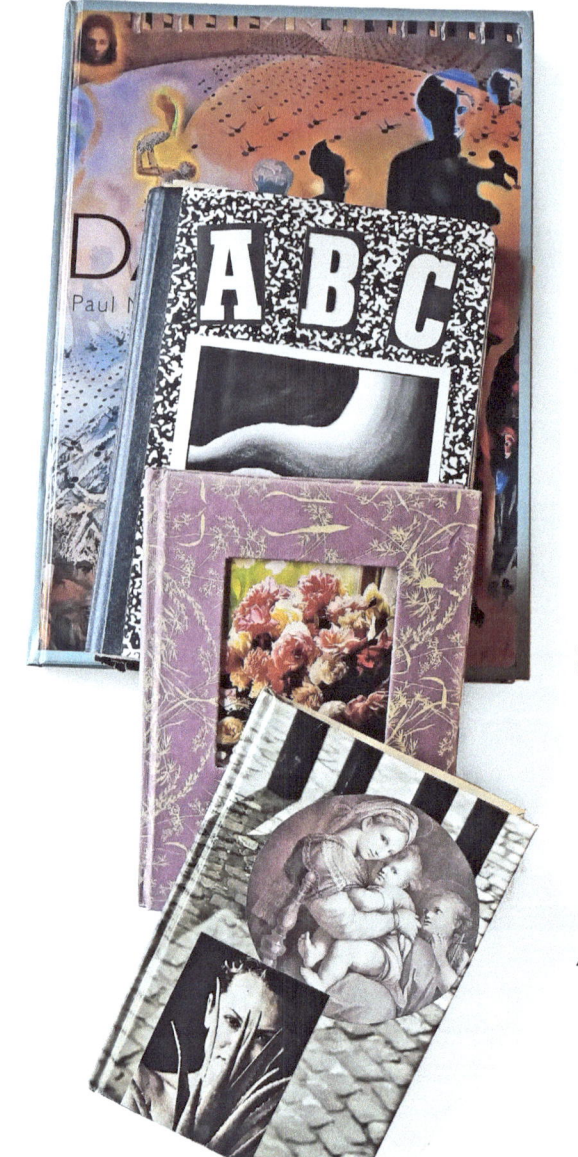

1.

2.

3.

4.

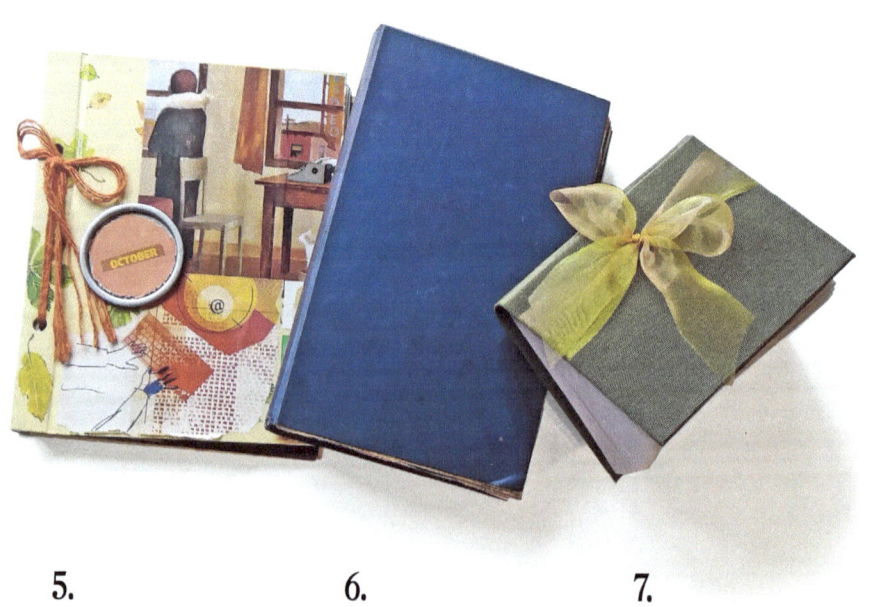

5.　　　　6.　　　　7.

My gluebooks, on the facing page:

1. An oversized art book that's roughly 14.5x10.5 inches when closed, and contains 100 pages. I usually glue two or three pages together when I work in this book. Also, the pages are glossy, which is not ideal.

2. A composition book with lined pages. This is your standard 100 page, 8x10 inch book. Lots of gluebookers start with these as their first book, because they're inexpensive and easy to find. Again, I glue two or three pages together when I work in this book.

3. A journal with blank handmade paper pages. This one is about 8.5x6 inches when closed, and contains 40 nice, heavy pages.

4. A journal with lined pages. This is one of those cheap journals with flimsy pages, designed to take notes or write your grocery list. I glue two or three pages together in this one, too.

5. A dollar store photo album. About 9x7 inches when closed. I replaced the original flimsy pages with cardstock. I like this kind of tie at the side book, because it's flexible. I can add as many pages as I need, and just tie it off when I think I'm done. There are 31 pages in this book, because I used it for an October daily page challenge.

6. An old thesaurus. About 9.5x6 inches when closed, and 500 pages. Although the paper is nice and heavy, I usually glue two together before I start working, and I also remove pages, so it won't splay open too much. (More about using old books as gluebooks later.)

7. A dollar store photo album, about 6.5x5 inches when closed, with 20 pages of plastic pockets to hold individual photos. I filled this with 4x6 inch gluecards. (More about gluecards later.)

What glue should I use?

Again, whatever you want to use. Most gluebookers have the best success with dry adhesives, like glue sticks, ATG tape, or rubber cement. I generally gluebook with large, clear glue sticks, even when I'm working on small projects.

While wet glues like Tacky or Elmers will also work, the wetter the glue, the longer the dry time. Also, wet glues increase the frequency of wrinkles, which some people dislike seeing on a finished page.

My suggestion is to start with a glue that you have, and already like.

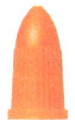

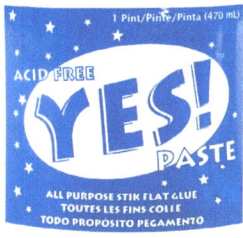

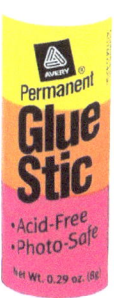

What stuff should I glue?

For the most part, anything you find, or have laying around. Rather than relying on papers, stickers and image sheets purchased for a page, gluebooking is best done with things that are the fallout from everyday life, like old magazines, receipts, junk mail, bills, and, well here, let me show you...

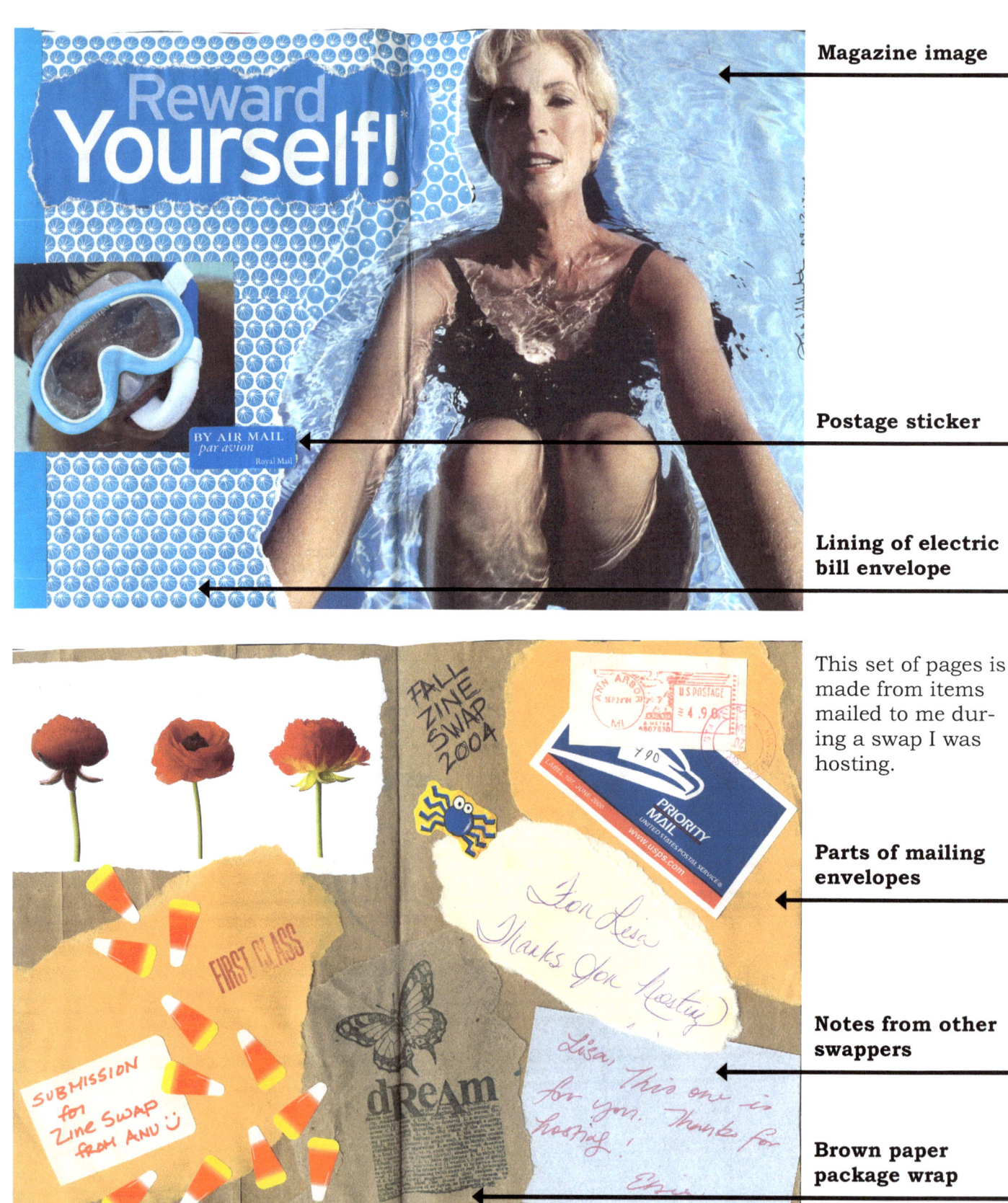

Magazine image

Postage sticker

Lining of electric bill envelope

This set of pages is made from items mailed to me during a swap I was hosting.

Parts of mailing envelopes

Notes from other swappers

Brown paper package wrap

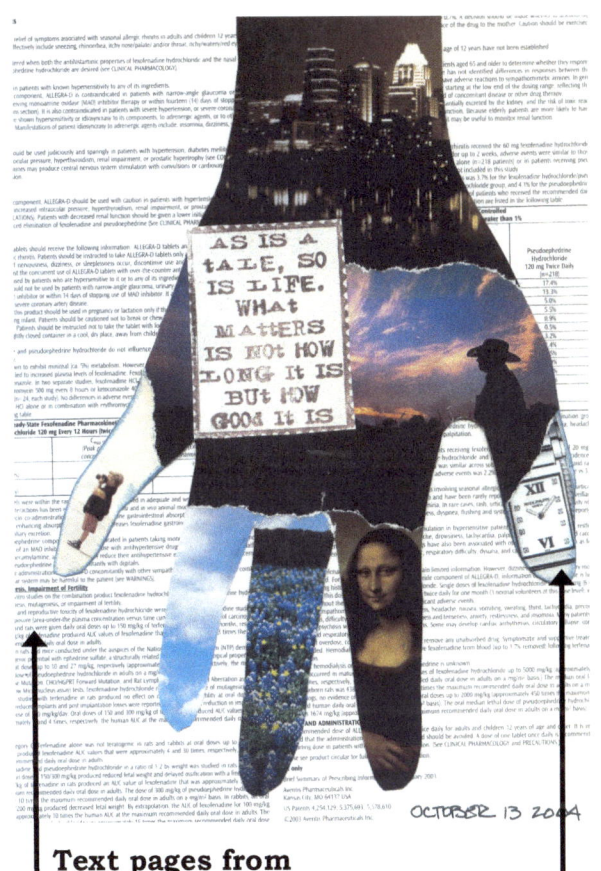

AS IS A TALE, SO IS LIFE. WHAT MATTERS IS NOT HOW LONG IT IS BUT HOW GOOD IT IS

OCTOBER 13 2004

Text pages from magazines and newspapers

Outline of my hand covered with magazine images

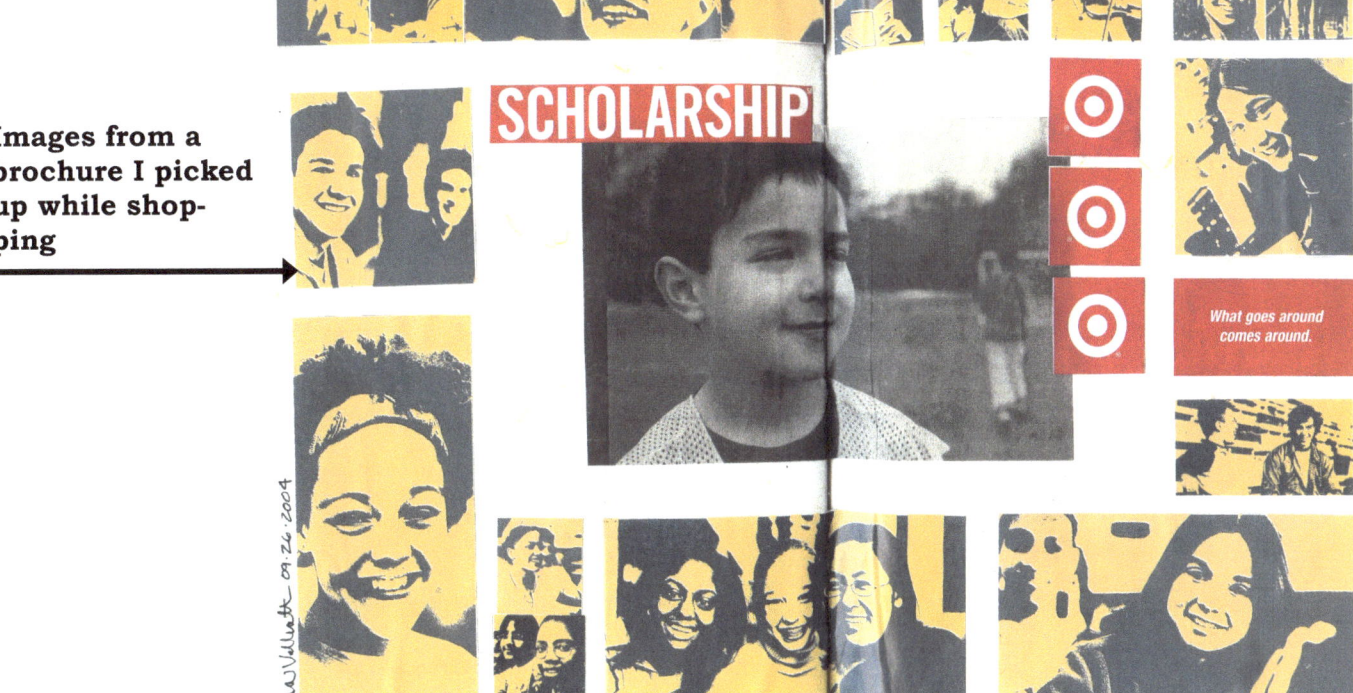

Ticket

$1.00

Faster

math

OCTOBER 23 2004

Paper scraps from another project

Stamps

Images from a brochure I picked up while shopping

SCHOLARSHIP

What goes around comes around.

How do I organize my images?

I know you can see this coming: in whatever way that works for you. I've seen people use file folders or envelopes to organize their images, or stacking file trays.

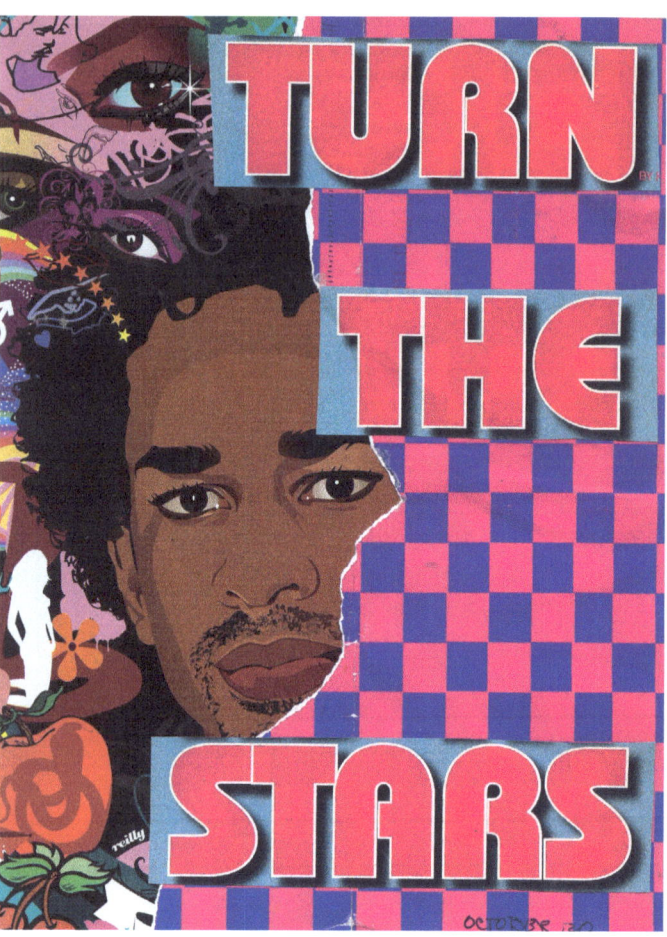

I don't organize my images at all, because I rarely remove them from their original publication until I'm ready to use them. When I'm ready to gluebook, I simply grab a couple of magazines, flip through them, and pull out anything that speaks to me in that particular moment. I find that more inspiring than cutting our every image and caption that catches my eye, and sifting through an envelope of them later.

What's a Smash Book?

Smash Books are a cross between a scrapbook and a junk journal They originally started with a line of products manufactured by K&Company, and because the idea is so product-focused, I'm not going to talk about them again, OK?

I will talk about junk journals, though, a little later in this book.

What's a vintage gluebook?

Vintage gluebooks are glued, using vintage and vintage inspired images and elements. Because the items that go into these books are purchased rather than found, they're not really gluebooks, so I'm not going to talk about these, either. The farthest I go down this road is to occasionally do a set of gluebook pages that uses vintage inspired photos from magazines.

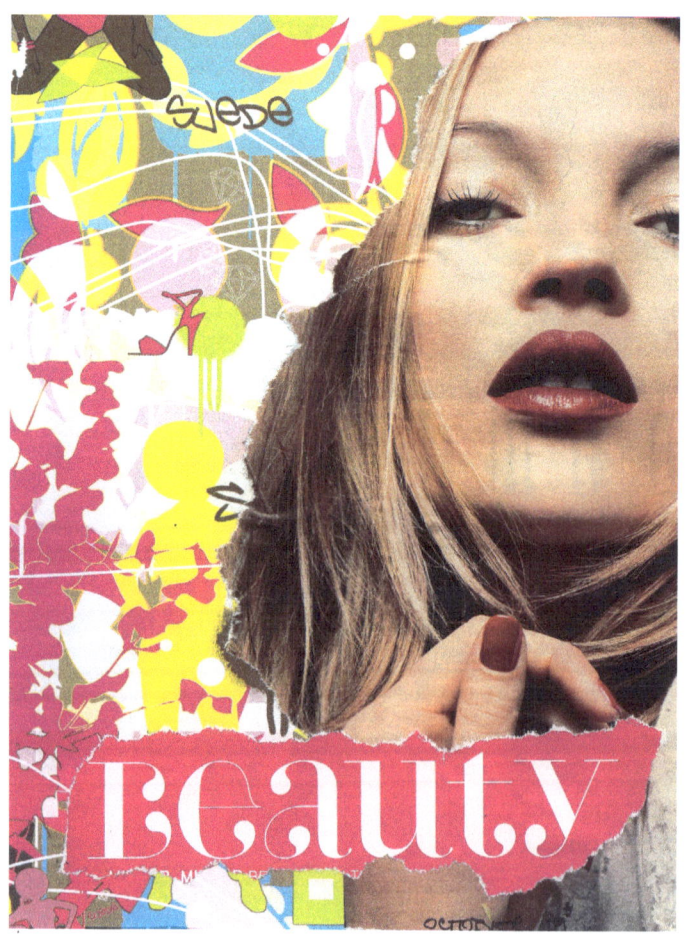

Gluebook Page by Andina Sling-van Bruggen

Wildervank, The Netherlands

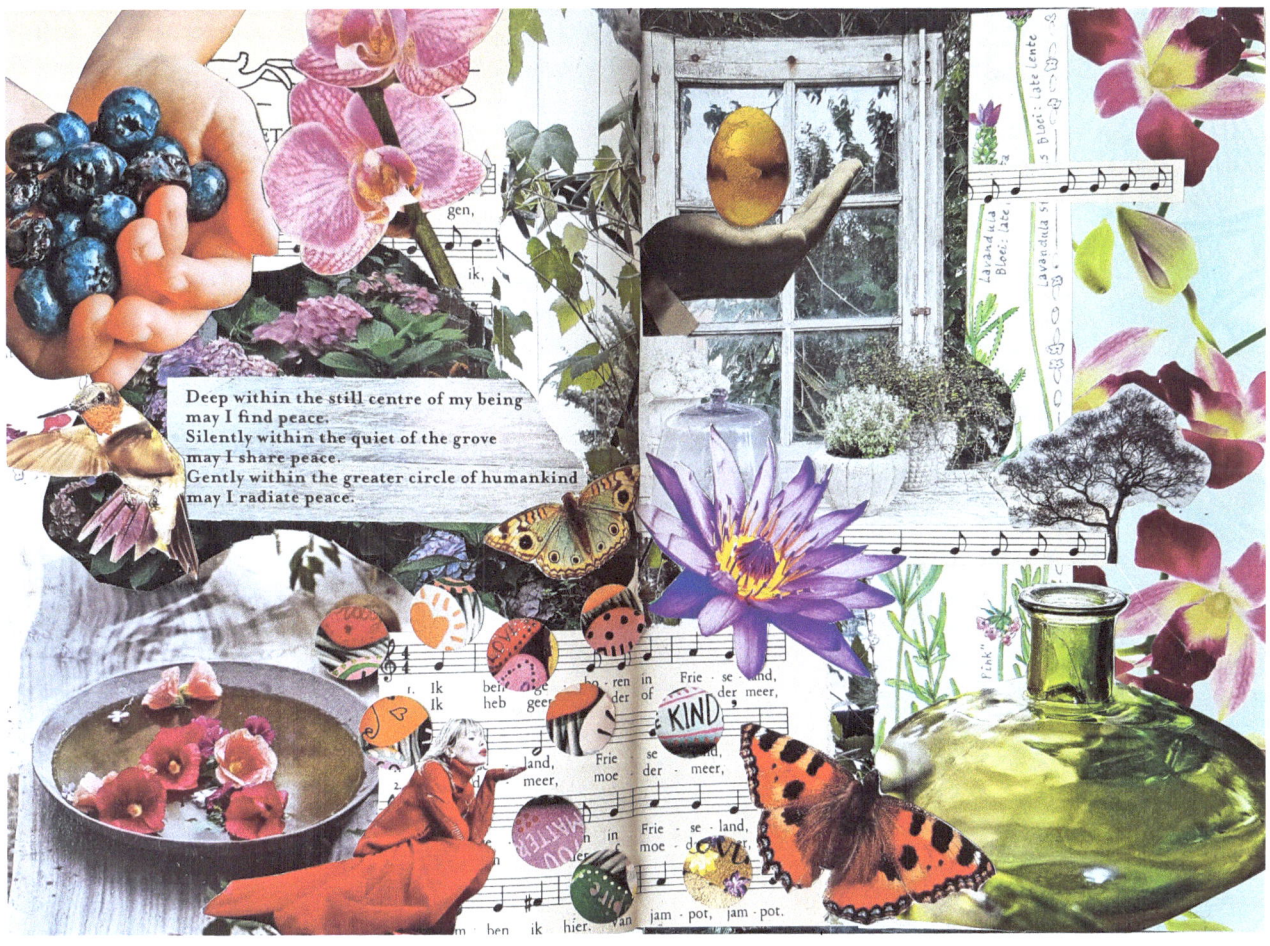

"I'm used to making collages combined with paint or other mixed media materials, but gluebooking is new to me.
I discovered this kind of collage on Facebook, Instagram and Pinterest."

Building Beautiful Pages

So, you've got a book, and some glue, and a pile of papery goodness. Now what?

Now, you cut and glue. Try not to think too much, or get too stressed out about what goes where, or whether your page is good. Gluebooking is all about developing your eye, and your instinctive knowledge that this piece looks good here, and this other one looks good with it. Each page you create will teach you something, and improve that creative eye.

Bonus: you don't have to worry about using up expensive supplies, or spending hours on end, only to have your pages turn into a disaster at the last minute. Just cut, and glue.

I know some of you immediately became apprehensive reading this. There's gotta be a right and wrong way to do this, right?

There isn't. Trust me. Gluebook pages are as varied as their creators. Whatever you want to do, or try, is fine. But for those of you who need a little more guidance than "whip out your gluestick and start", I've filled the next handful of pages with some ideas about how to build your beautiful gluebook pages, so you'll have a place to start.

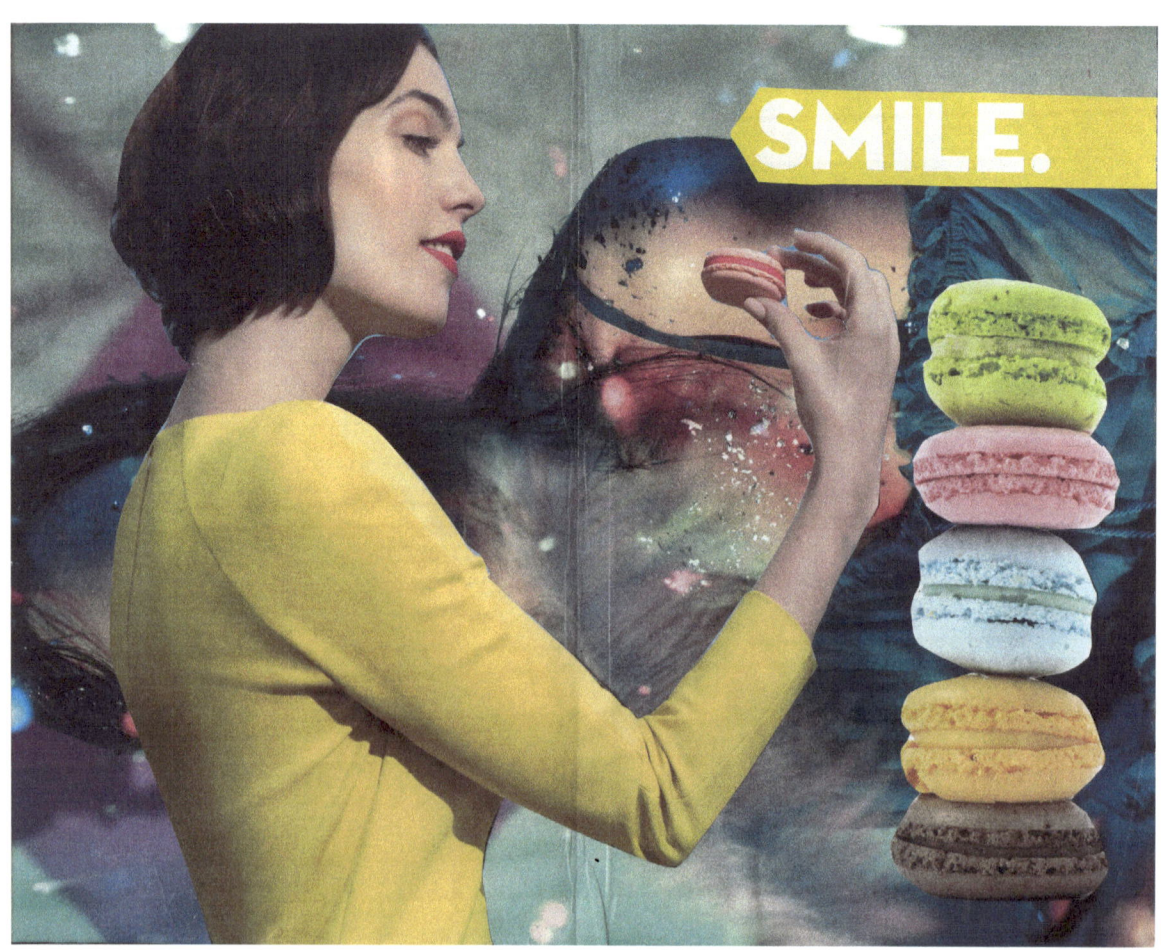

Single pages or double?

Gluebooks can be decorated on one side, or both sides of a page layout. If you prefer your work with a portrait orientation, work single pages. If landscape is more your style, work double.

I tend to let the book I'm using dictate whether I work single or double. Spiral bound book? Single page, because that spiral is in the way of doing double gracefully. Old dictionary? Single or double, because the undecorated dictionary pages make an unobtrusive facing page for my artwork. Comp book? Probably double, because those lines showing will drive me a little nuts.

This is another decision that's totally up to you. There isn't a wrong answer. Work the way you feel comfortable.

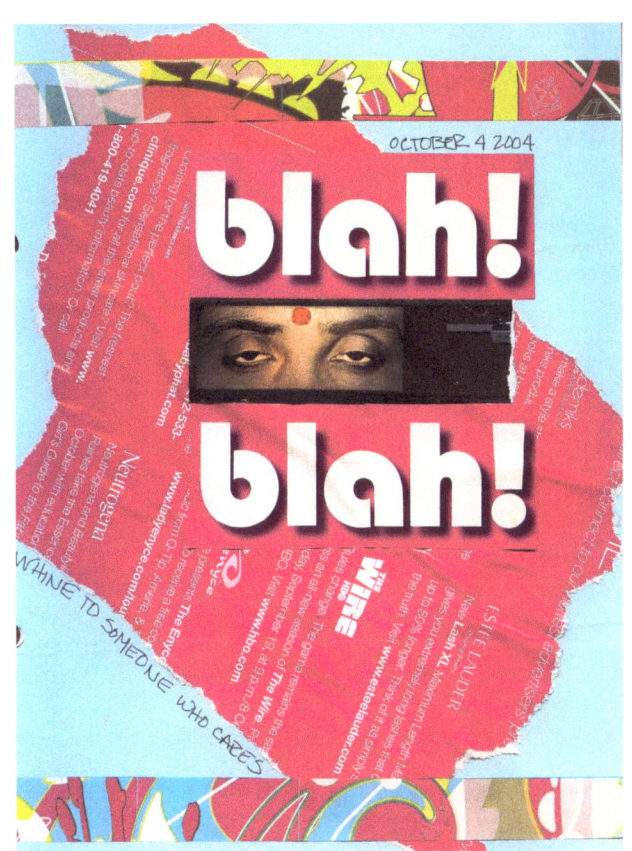

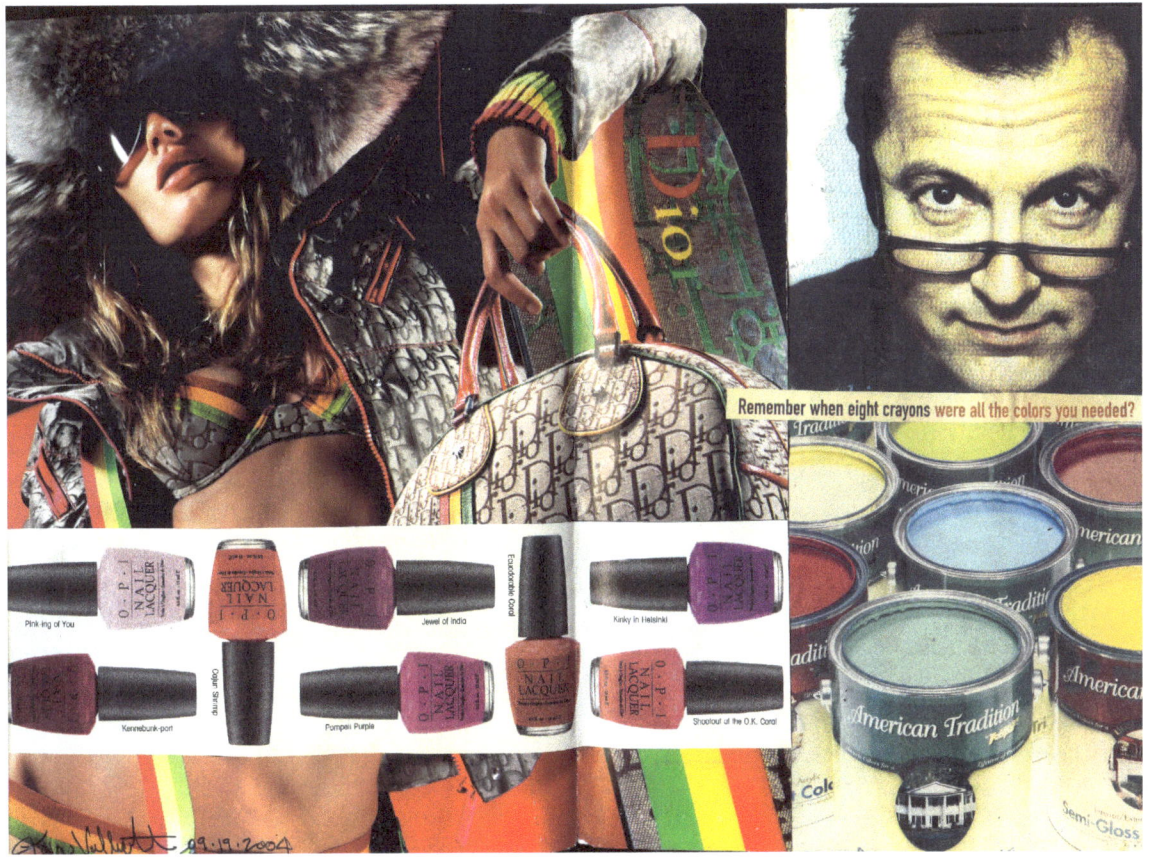

Telling a Story

In every class I teach, no matter what type of artwork I'm showing how to create, I like to talk a little bit about telling a story. I like to approach my artwork as a visual storyteller, and gluebooks allow me to tell lots of little stories, very quickly.

So, what's a story? One or two words, or even a sentence, that sums up what I'm trying to convey visually. Let's give it a try, with some of my gluebook pages:

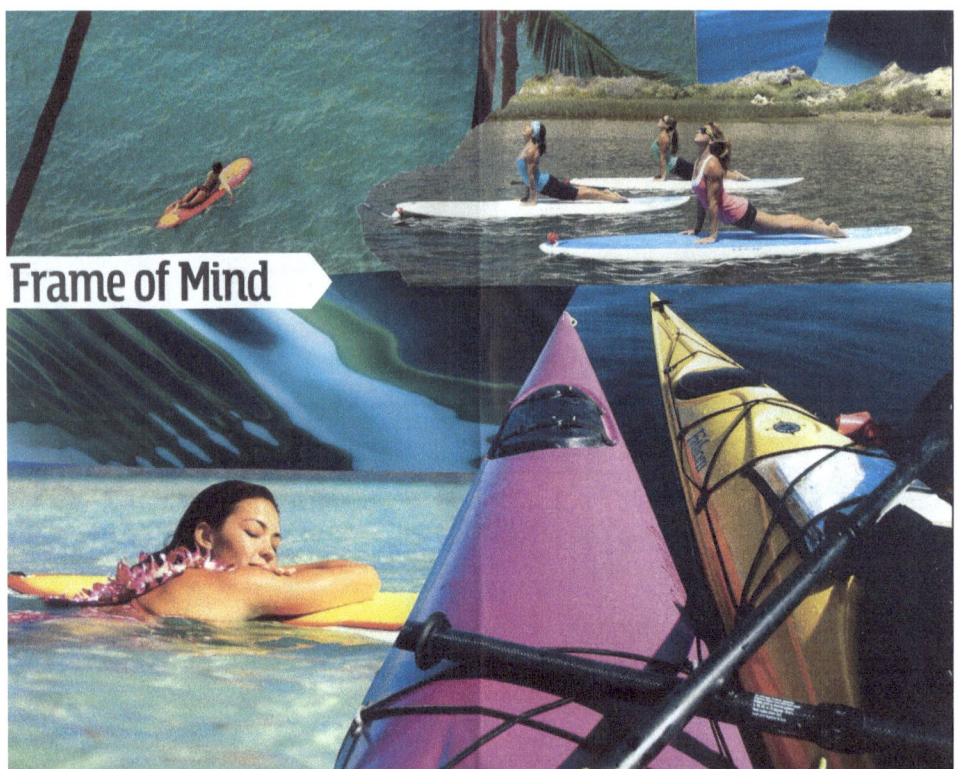

My story here is pretty simple. Water. Calm. Aqua and blue.

I think this is probably a story that would be obvious to any viewer. They would think one of those words I gave as my story.

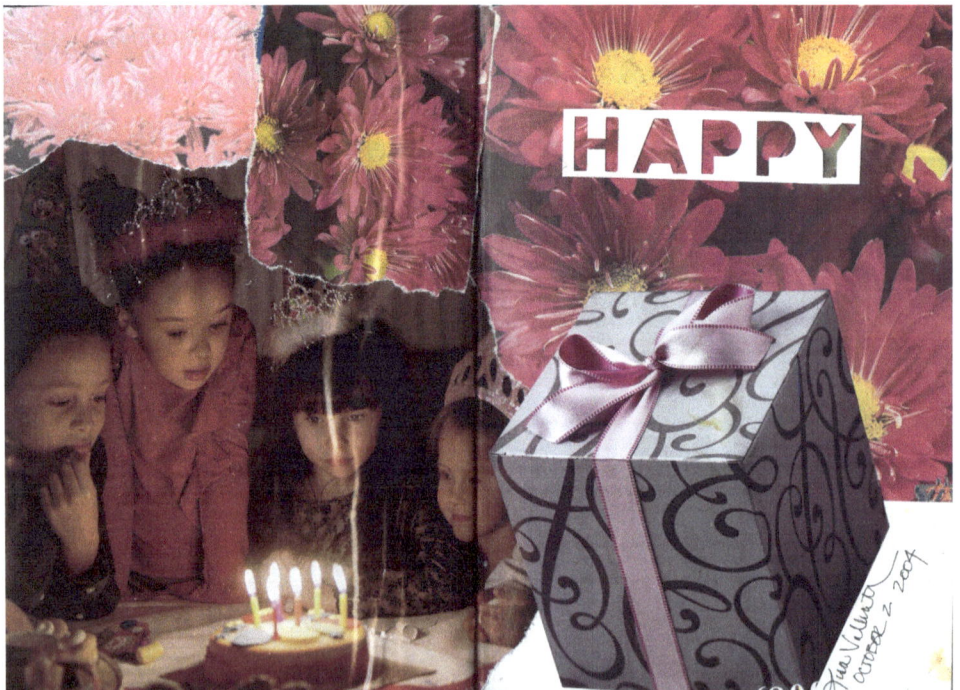

Here's a set of pages I did on my birthday. My story here: birthday, and pink.

Did you get that when you looked at it? If so, I was successful at conveying my story. If not, maybe the elements say something else to you, and that's OK, too. Just because I have a story in my head doesn't mean everyone will see what I do, or what you do. Sometimes, stories are obvious, and sometimes they're not.

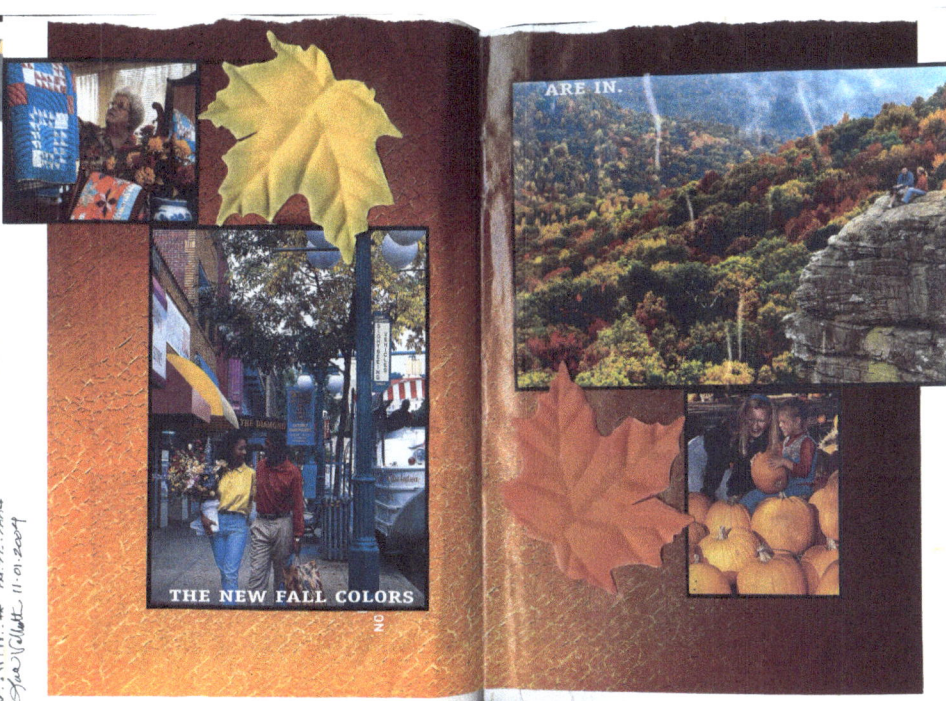

I'll bet you looked at this one, and immediately said "autumn". That's the story I was telling with these pages.

This story is a little more complicated. I had in mind a dark, modern Cinderella. The girl in the dress with the big up-do, the clock, and the strange pumpkins were the elements I thought might indicate that story.

Did you get Cinderella from this when you first looked at it? No? That's OK. Not every story has to be as obvious to the viewer as my first example. Not every set of pages has to be easy to understand, or have an un-complicated idea behind it.

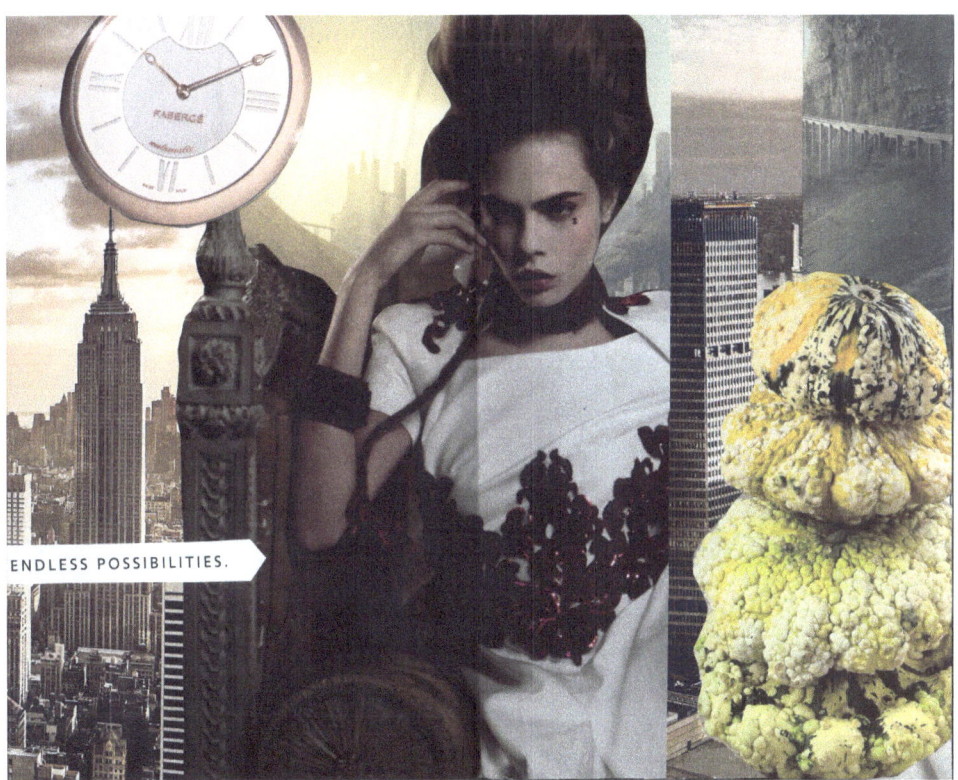

Telling a story happens whether you think of the words ahead of time or not. Sometimes, you might start gluing, and halfway through, realize your pages are heading in a direction you can put into words, and that becomes your story. Or maybe, you just glue a bunch of stuff, and someone else comes by, and says what they see, and you realize that's your story.

After you've gluebooked for a while, you'll know what you're trying to say before you start, or as you are pulling the elements of the page together. You'll instinctively know whether adding an ad-ditional piece helps or hinders the idea you're trying to convey. That's storytelling.

Color Themed Pages

One of the easiest ways of getting started on a gluebook page is to flip through a few magazines, and pull out images of a single color or combination of colors.

Start by pulling out images that are black and white, because most magazines have a lot of those. Put together a few that tell a story, and keep an eye out for larger images that might work as backgrounds.

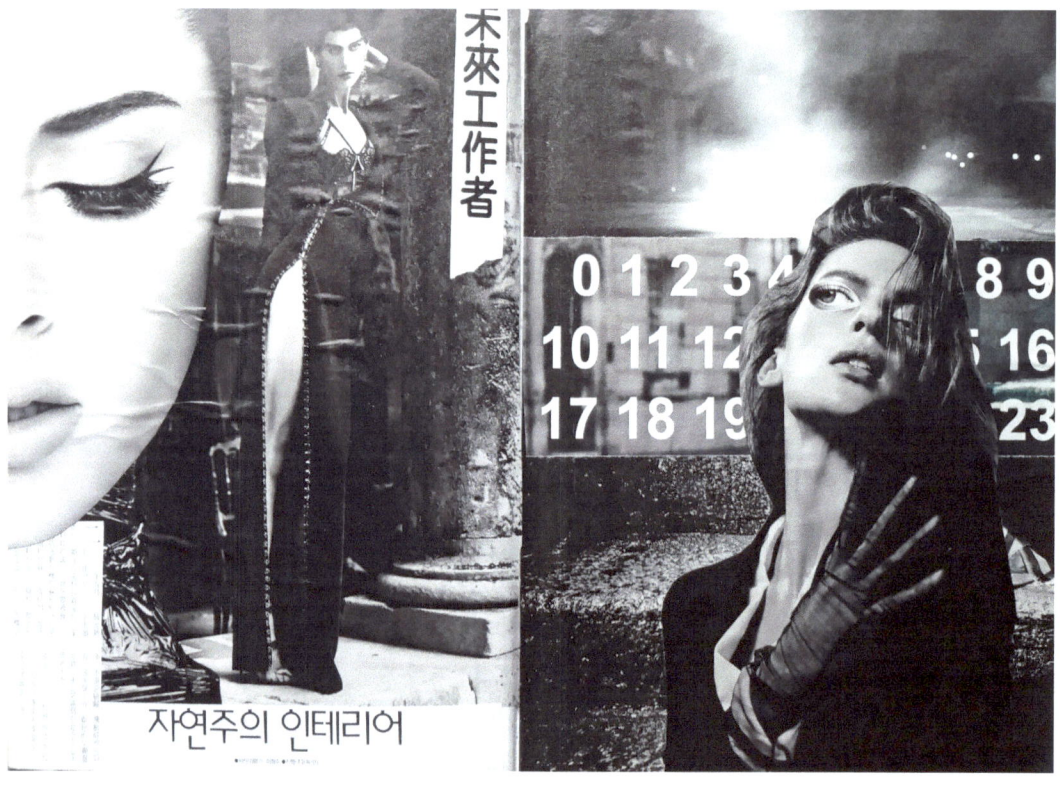

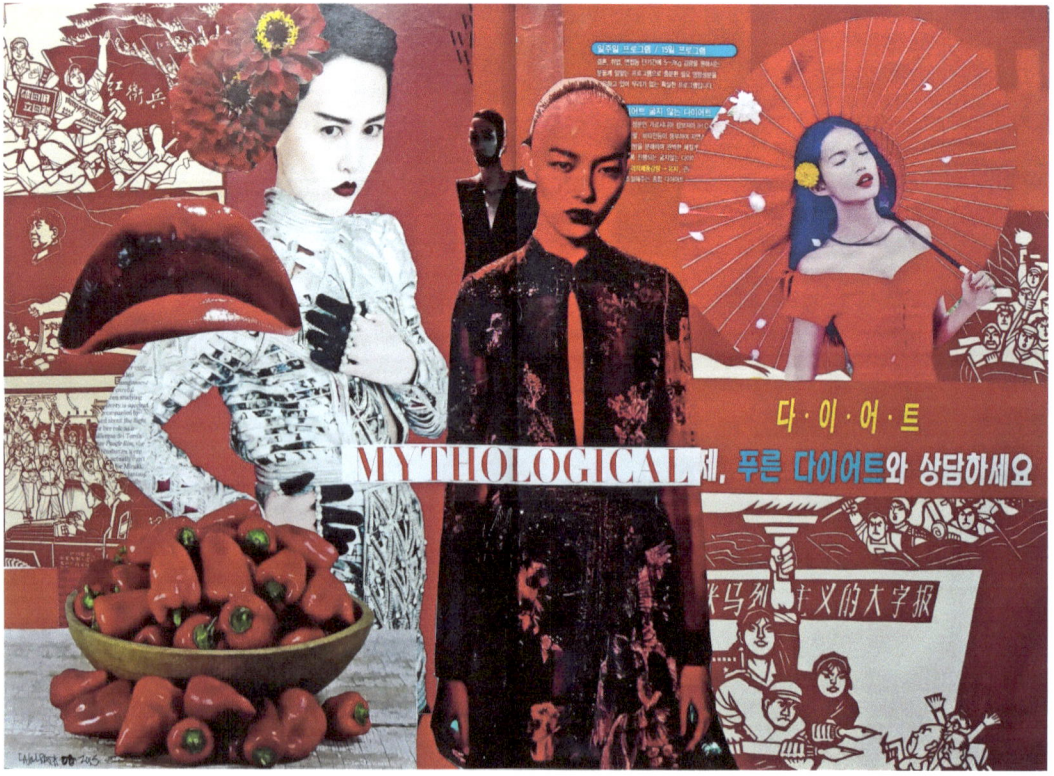

The gluebook pages shown here are from my largest book, which is about 15 inches tall. It's easy to get very complex compositions going by working on a larger set of pages. I find myself using more images, and obviously, larger ones, working on big pages. Backgrounds often have to be pieced from several pages, making them more visually interesting.

Building pages based on color is a great way to start gluebooking, because you don't have to think too much. If it's blue, it's in. If it's not, it's out. What could be easier?

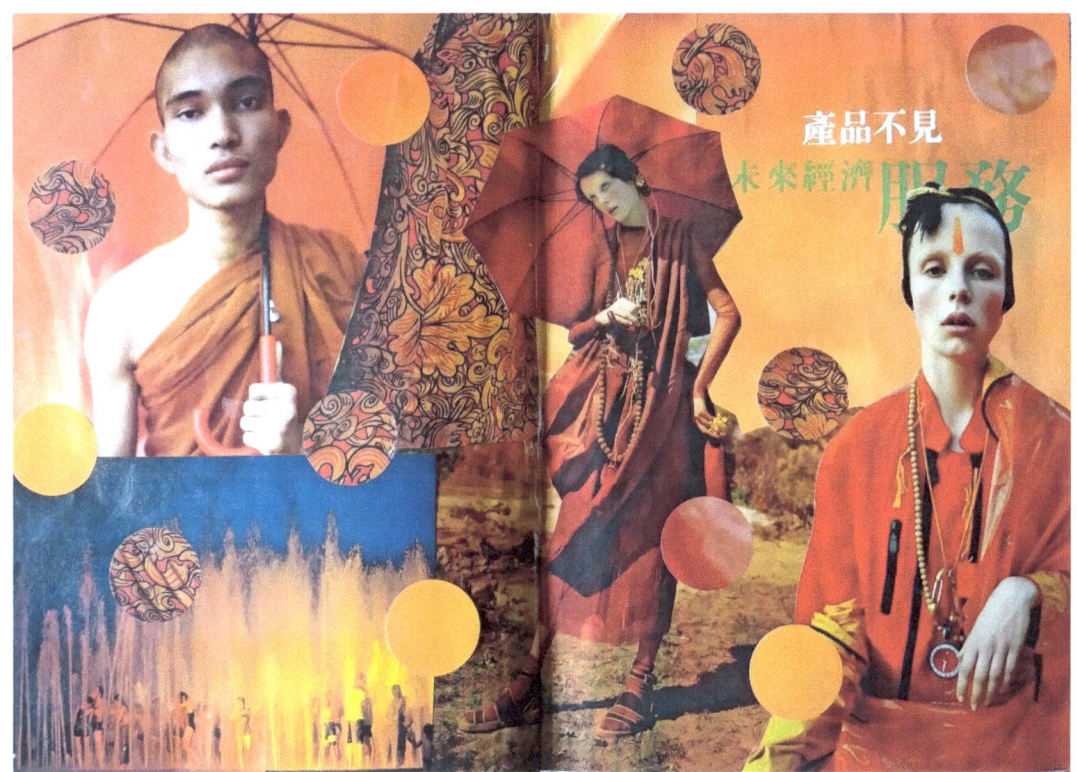

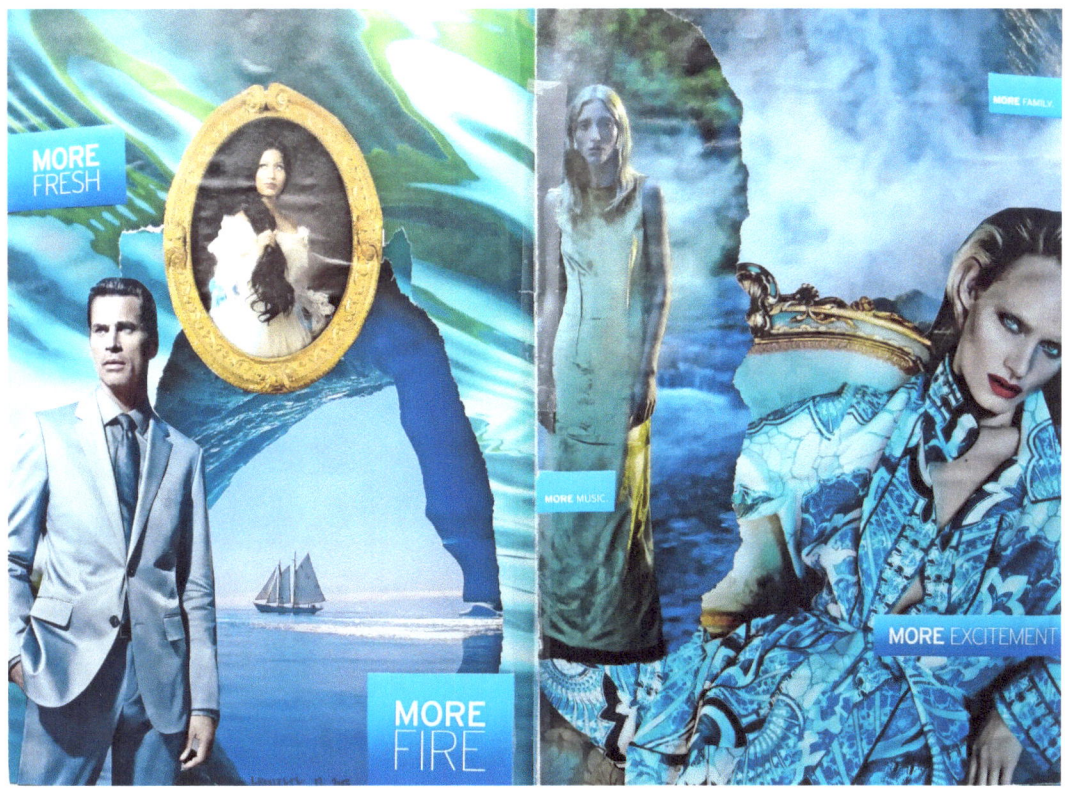

Building Pages Using Blocks

Another easy way to create gluebook pages is to simply work with blocks. Fill your space with images that relate to each other, or mean something to you. Work with blocks of color, or cut up pieces to create a sort of tiled mosaic.

Try varying the sizes of your images, rather than making each block the same size, to give your pages more visual interest.

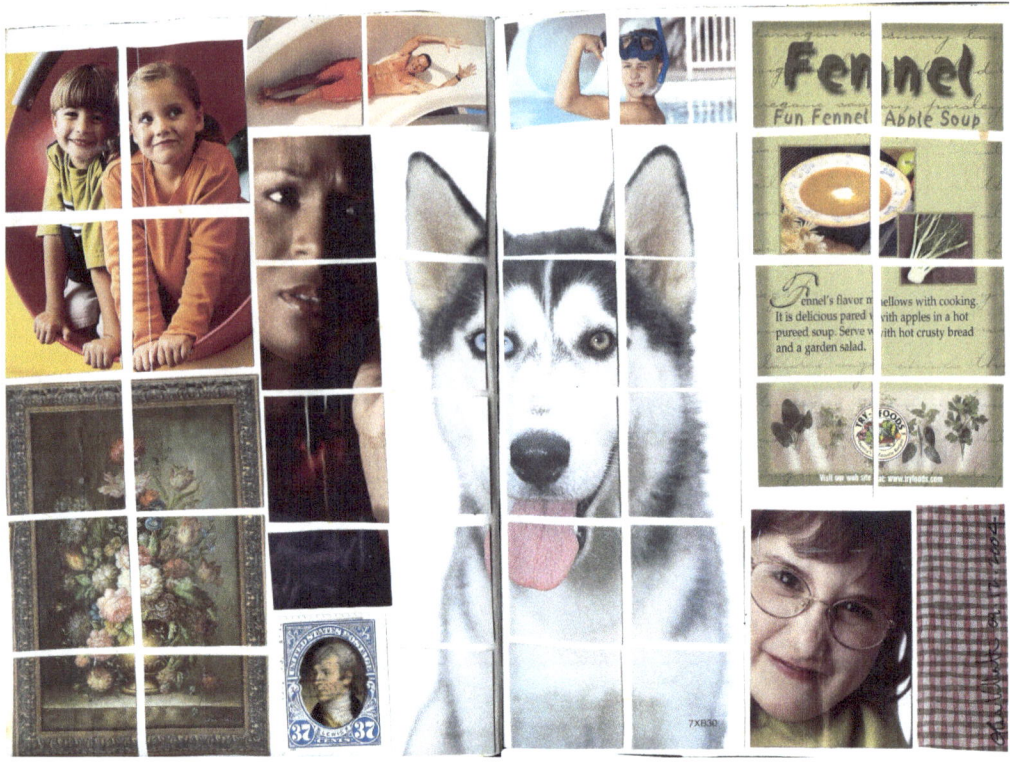

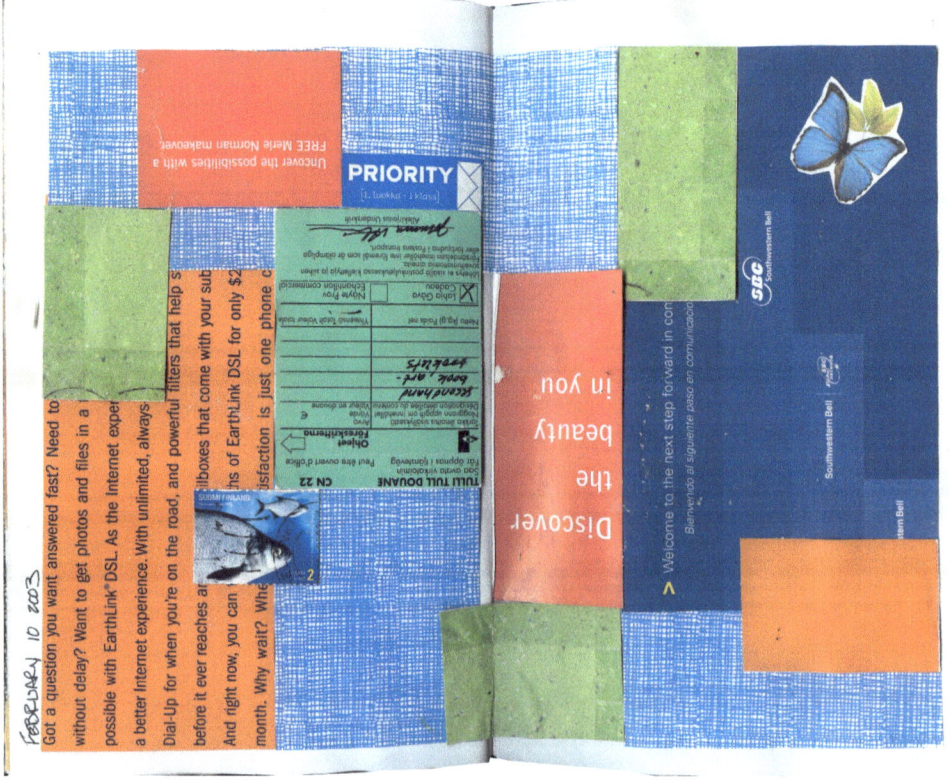

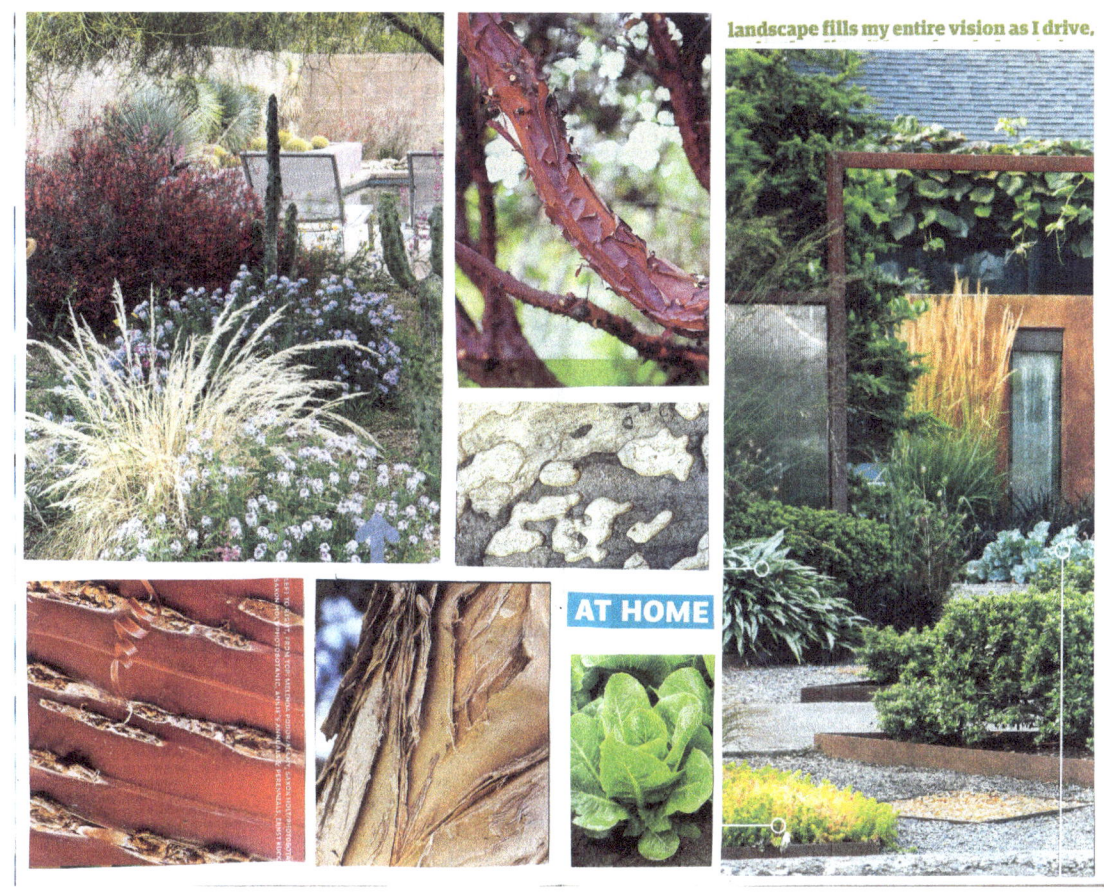

landscape fills my entire vision as I drive,

AT HOME

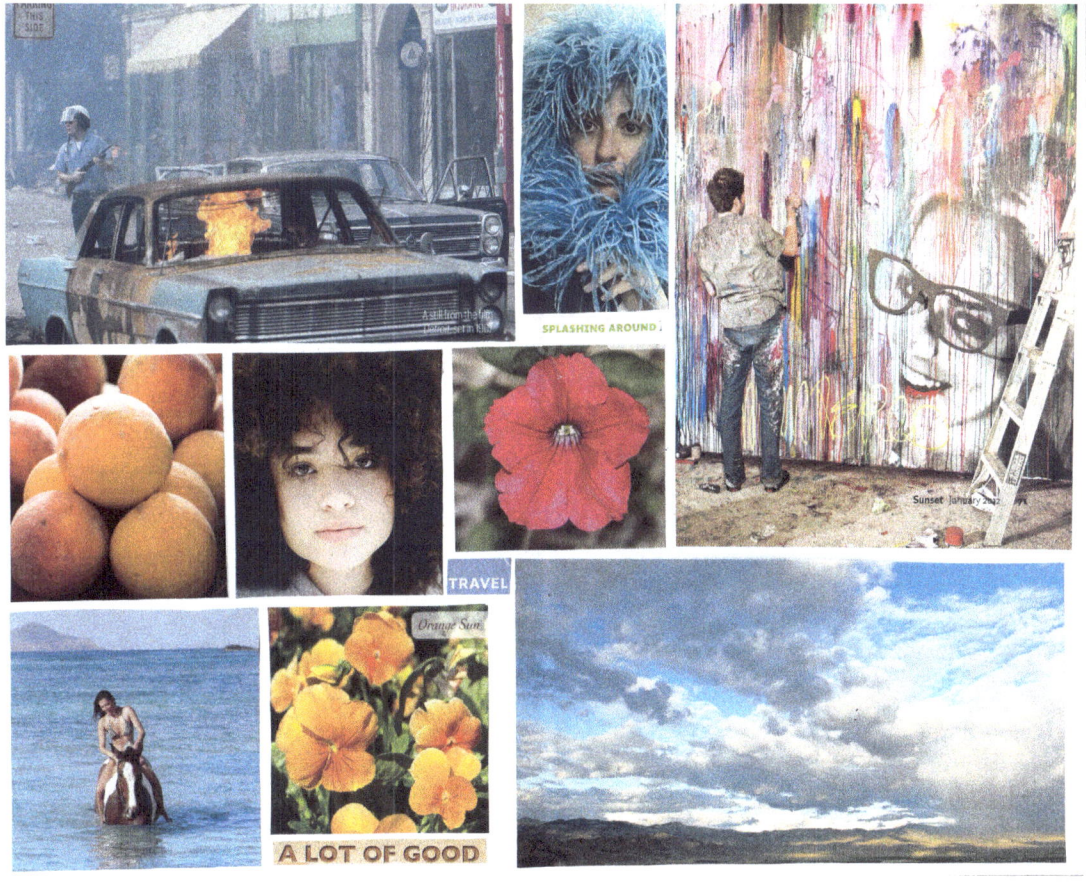

SPLASHING AROUND

TRAVEL

Orange Sun

A LOT OF GOOD

Adding a Little Punch

Do you have paper punches? Get some extra mileage out of them when you gluebook, by using them to create embellishments from whatever pile of papers you're working from today.

I often pull solid color magazine pages from fashion magazines to use with punches. If you're punching magazine pages, you'll want to do several layers at a time, because most punches will tear right through a single layer, and make a messy shape.

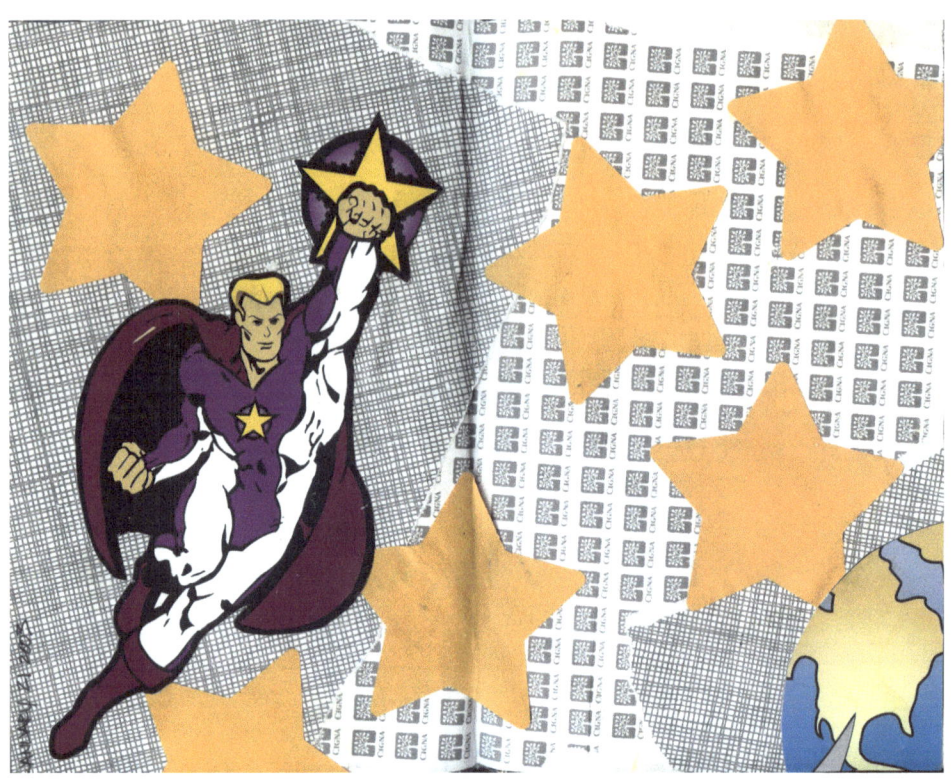

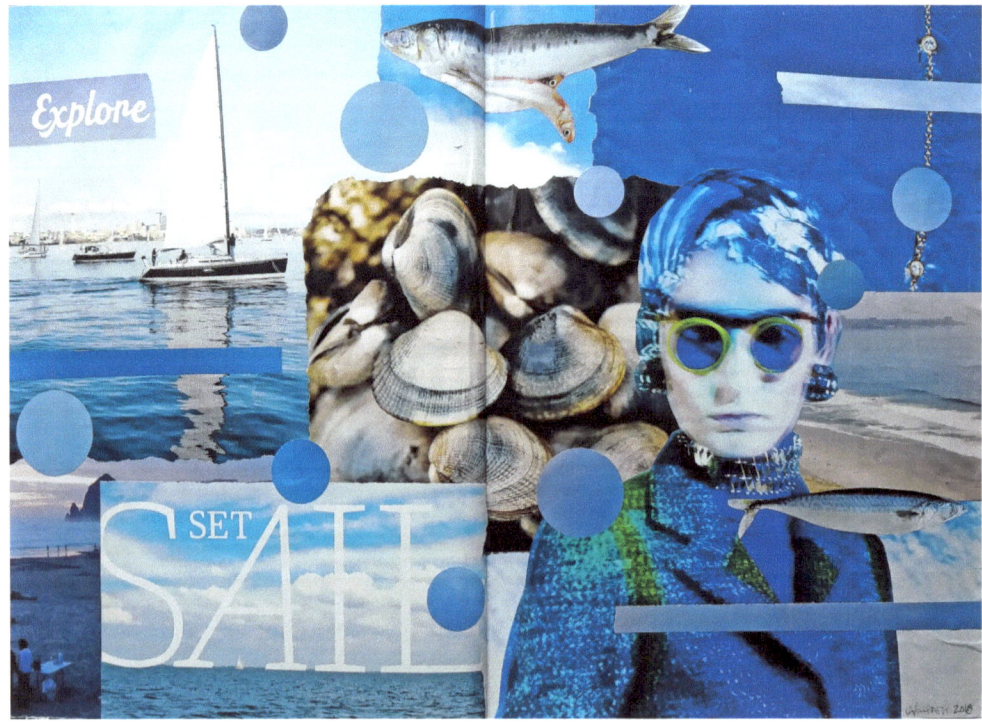

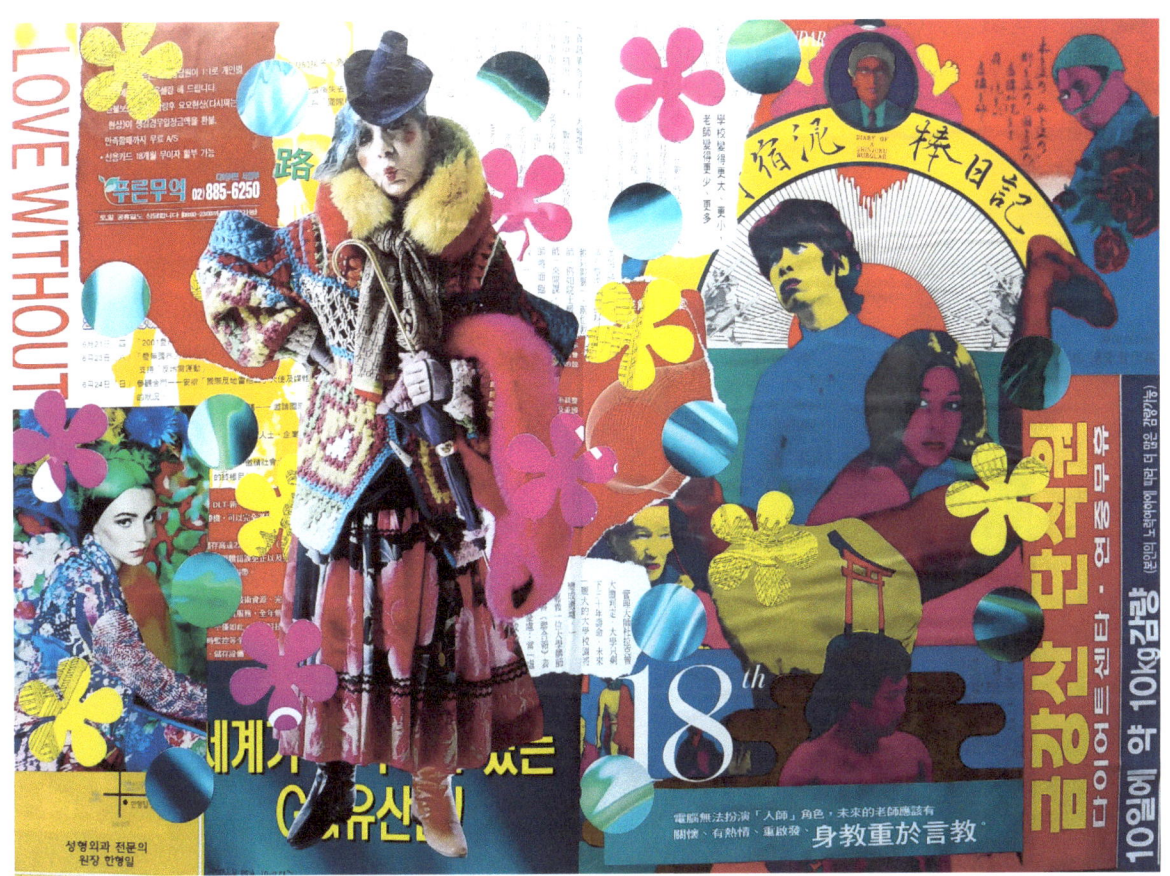

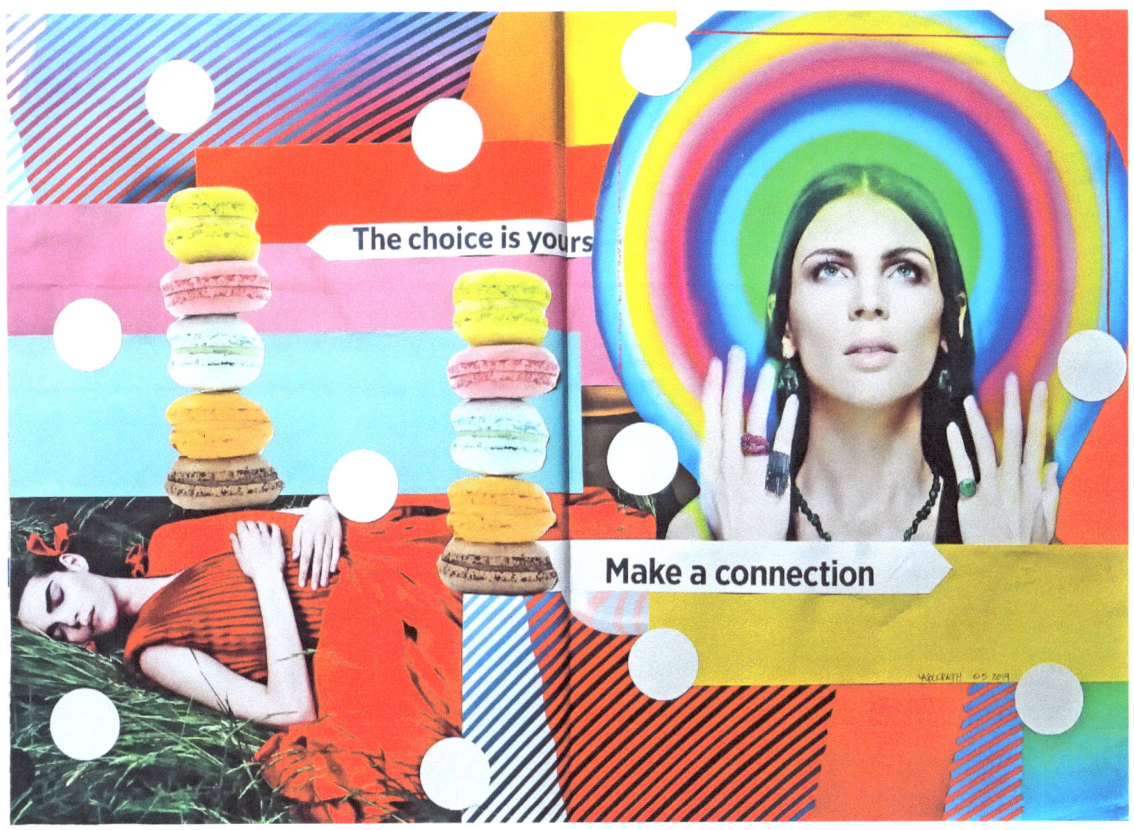

Adding Doodles

I am often asked of it's OK to draw in gluebooks. Of course it is! As long as you're focused on creating with what you have laying around, rather than acquiring more stuff you don't need, it's fine to grab a pen or two, and some doodles to complete your pages.

I generally use black Sharpies in various sizes to doodle on my pages. A white paint pen, or gel pen, is also handy. I try to limit myself to those two colors, so I'm not tempted to turn my pages into anything too complicated. I like to keep my pages quick and simple.

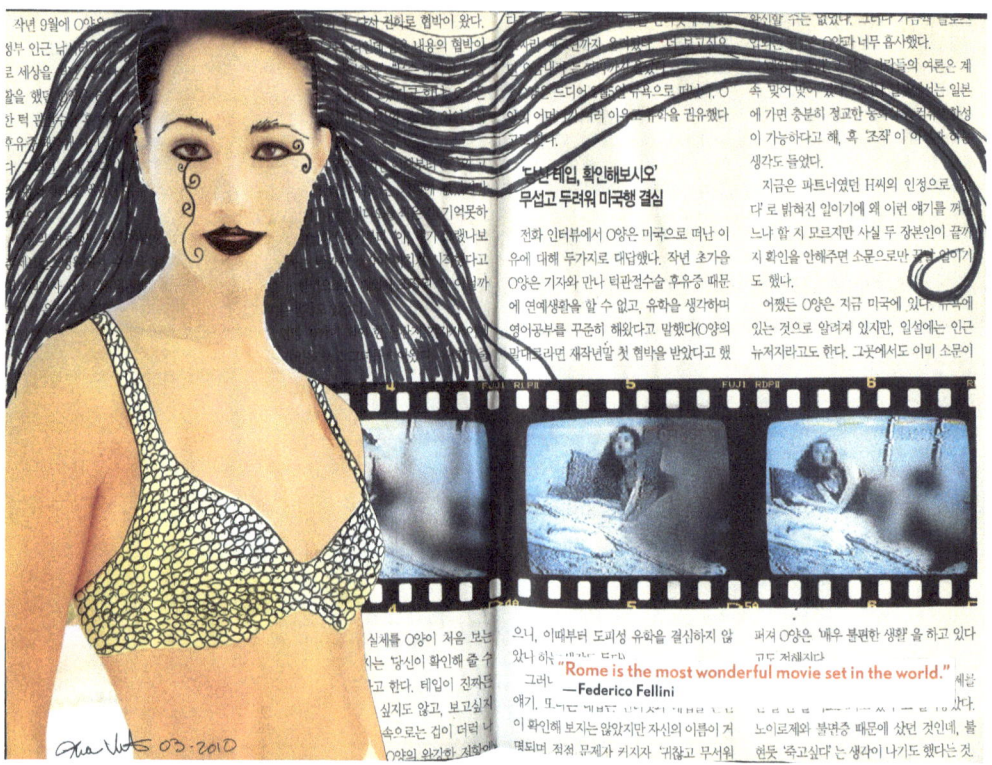

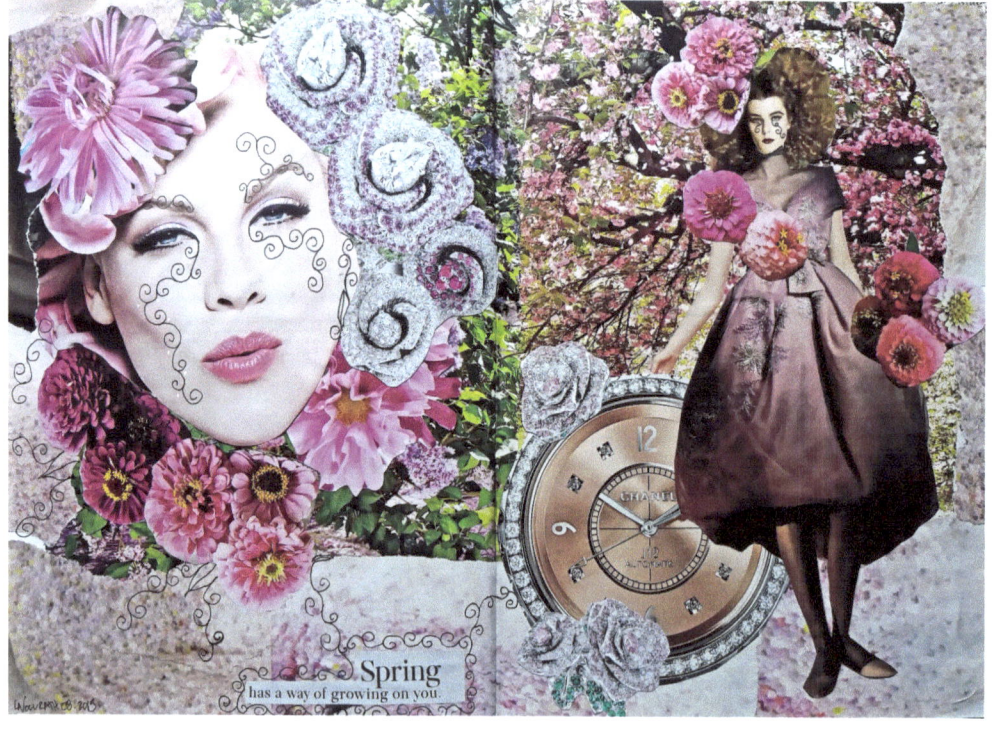

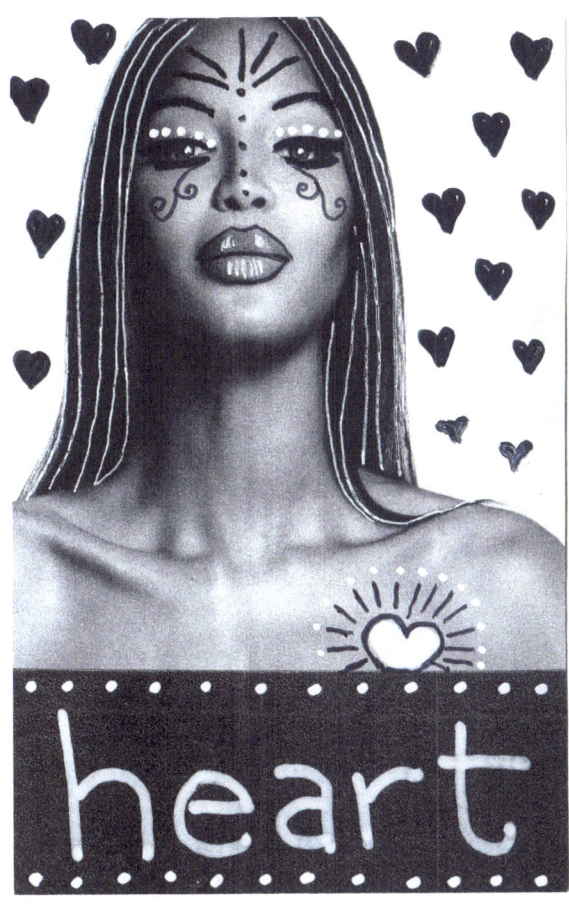

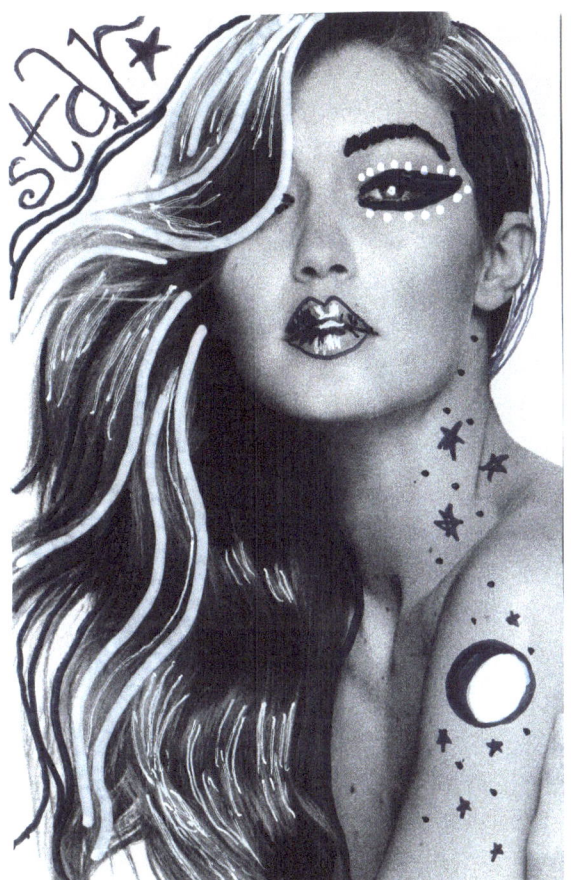

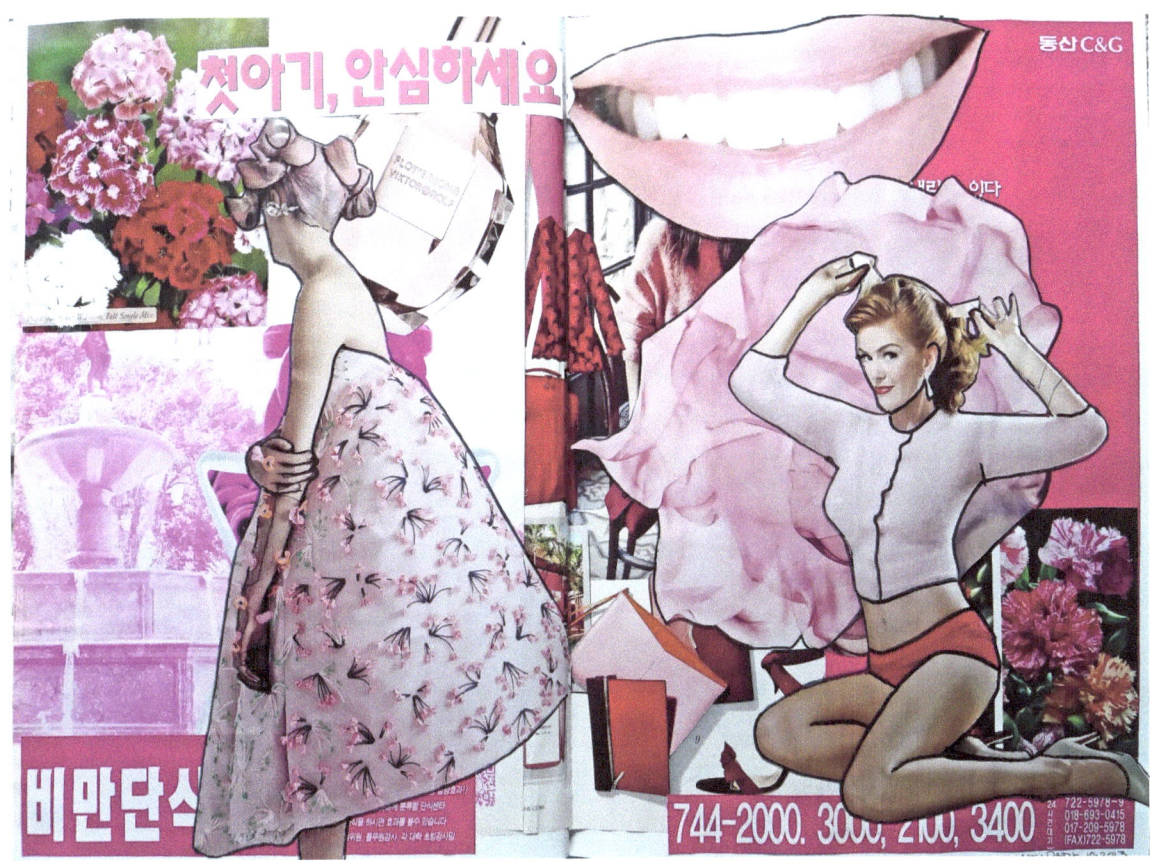

Creating Silly Characters

This is something sort of inspired by the strange and wonderful journal pages that Teesha Moore creates: whimsical figures, created from pieces and parts that don't have much to do with necks or bodies. For these gluecards, I used magazine images as backgrounds, and also as patterned papers, from which I cut curved shapes, stars, hearts and crowns. Combining those pieces with heads cut from ads, I created my whimsical characters.

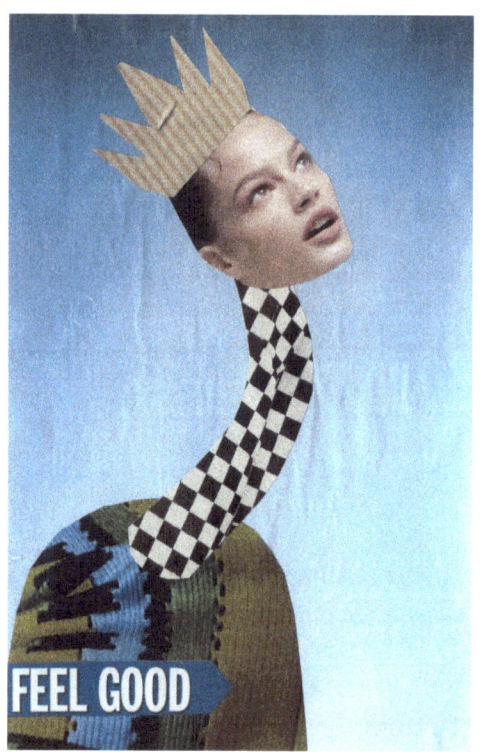

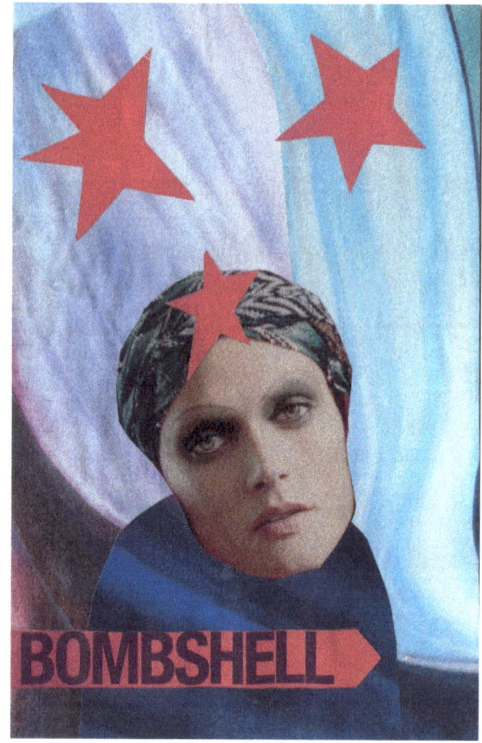

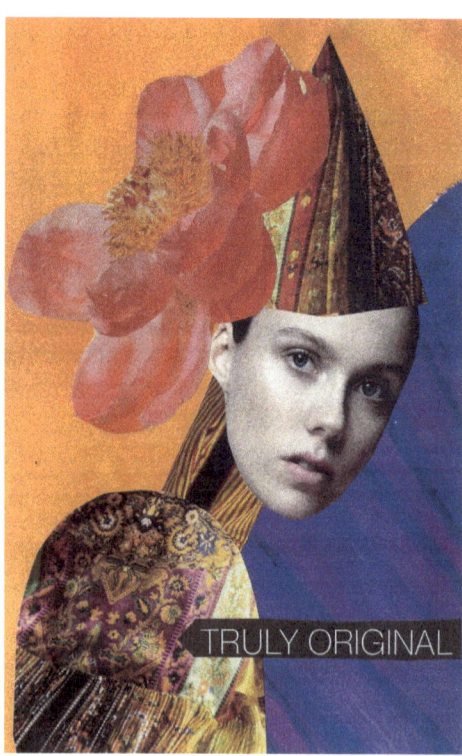

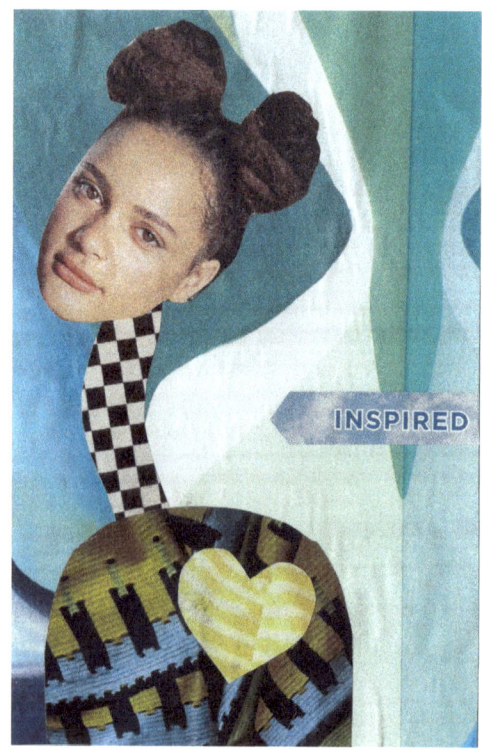

Using Gluebooks as Journals

If some of the paper ephemera you collect is from a special day out, or a vacation, gluebook pages can act as a sort of cross between scrapbook pages and journals, to record your experiences. The pages below were done after a trip to see the Turner in Venice exhibit at a local museum, and after seeing Cirque du Soleil. A few magazine pages, and a little doodling, added to the ticket stubs and other ephemera I brought home were all I needed to create pages to remind me of what I saw.

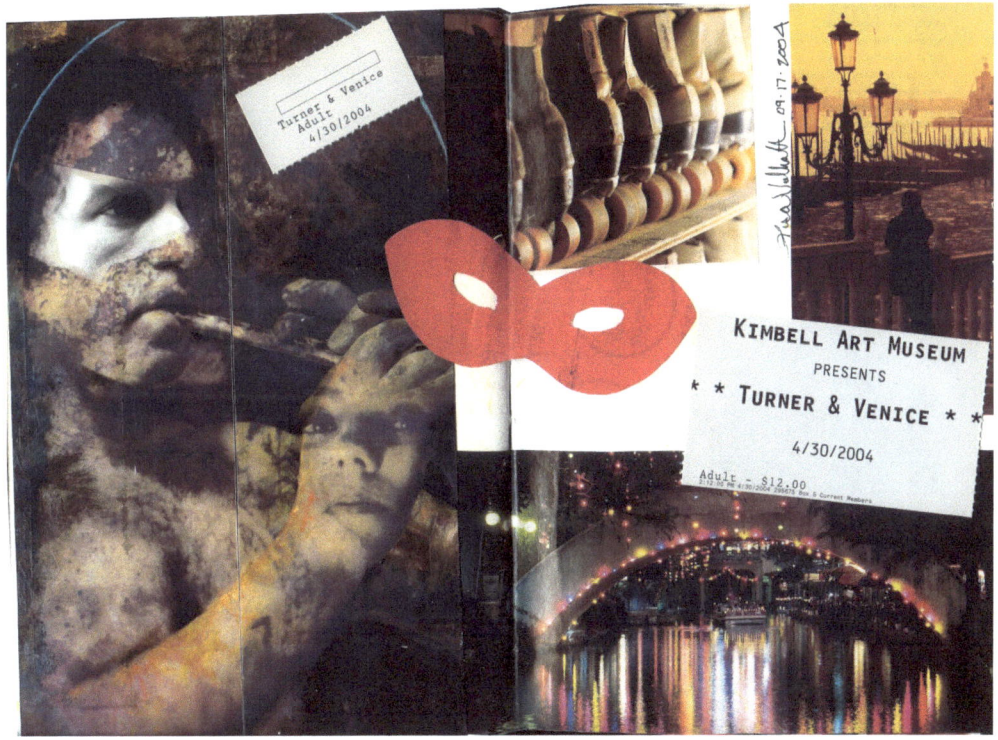

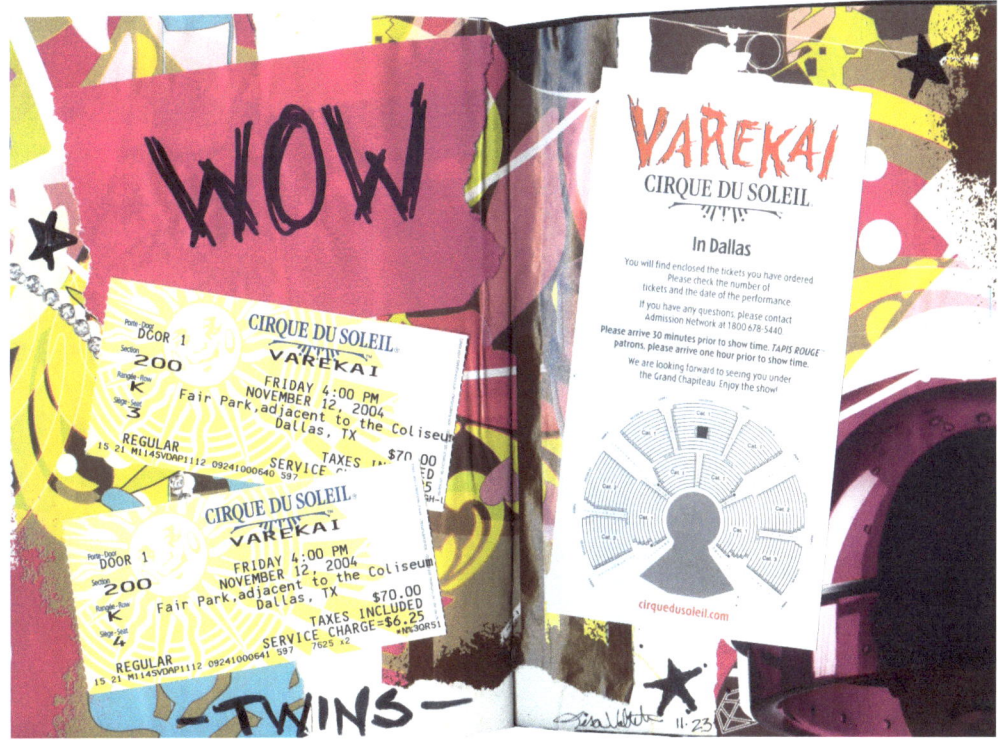

Gluebook Pages by Margaret Richardson

Olympia, Washington

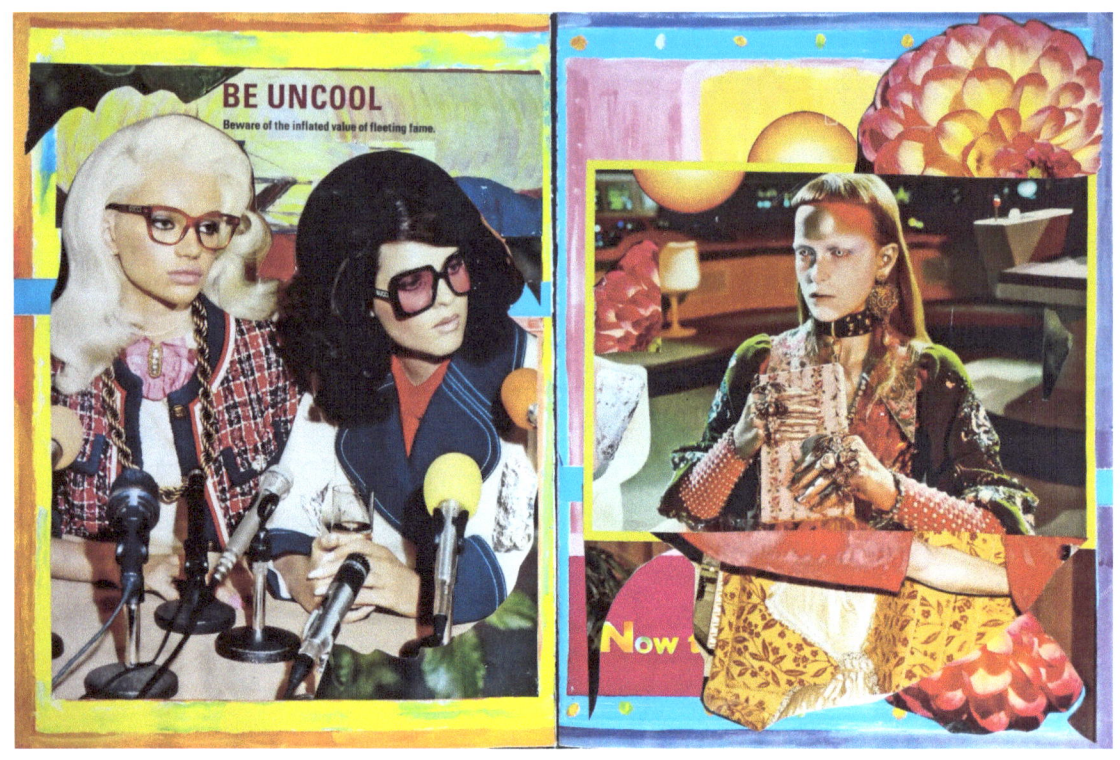

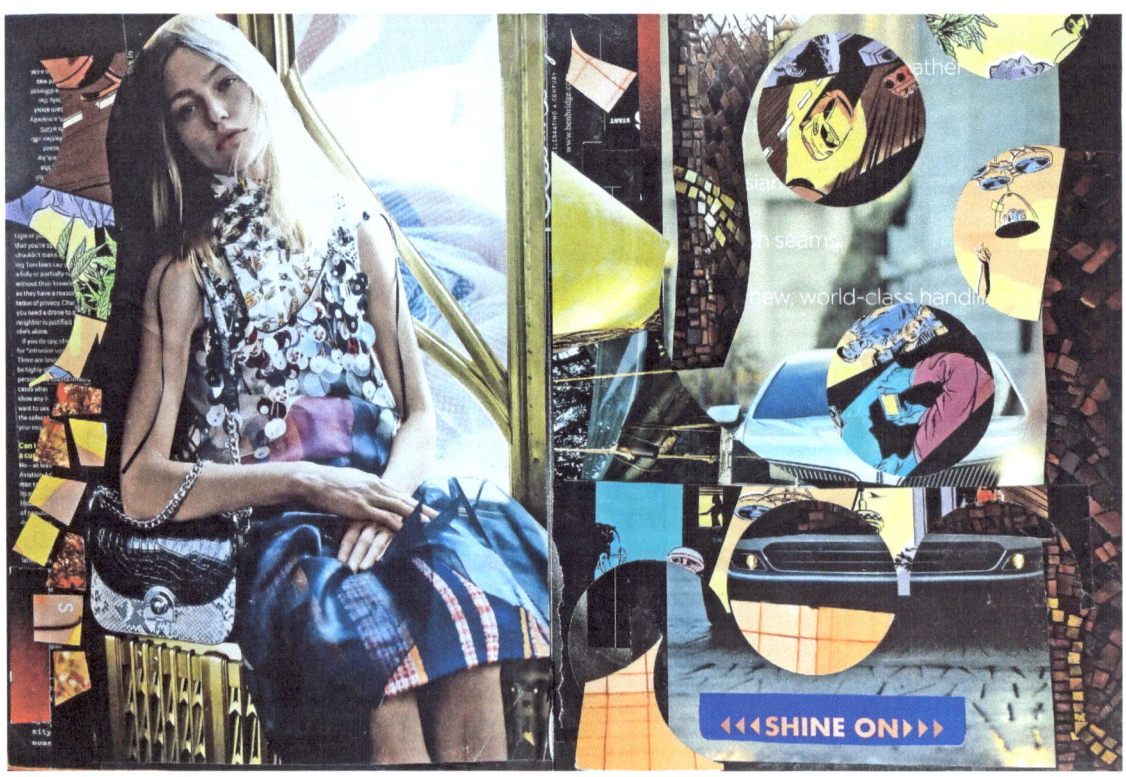

"I heard about gluebooking from Lisa.
It's fun and can be challenging at the same time."

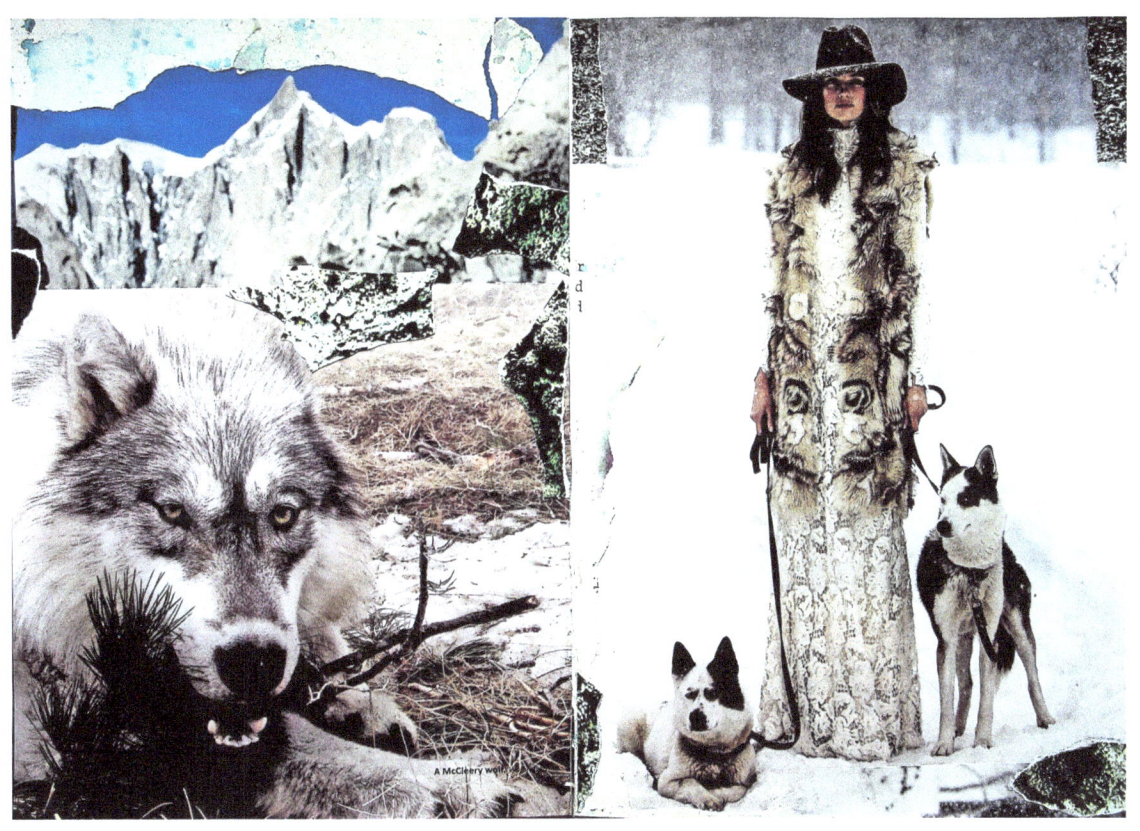

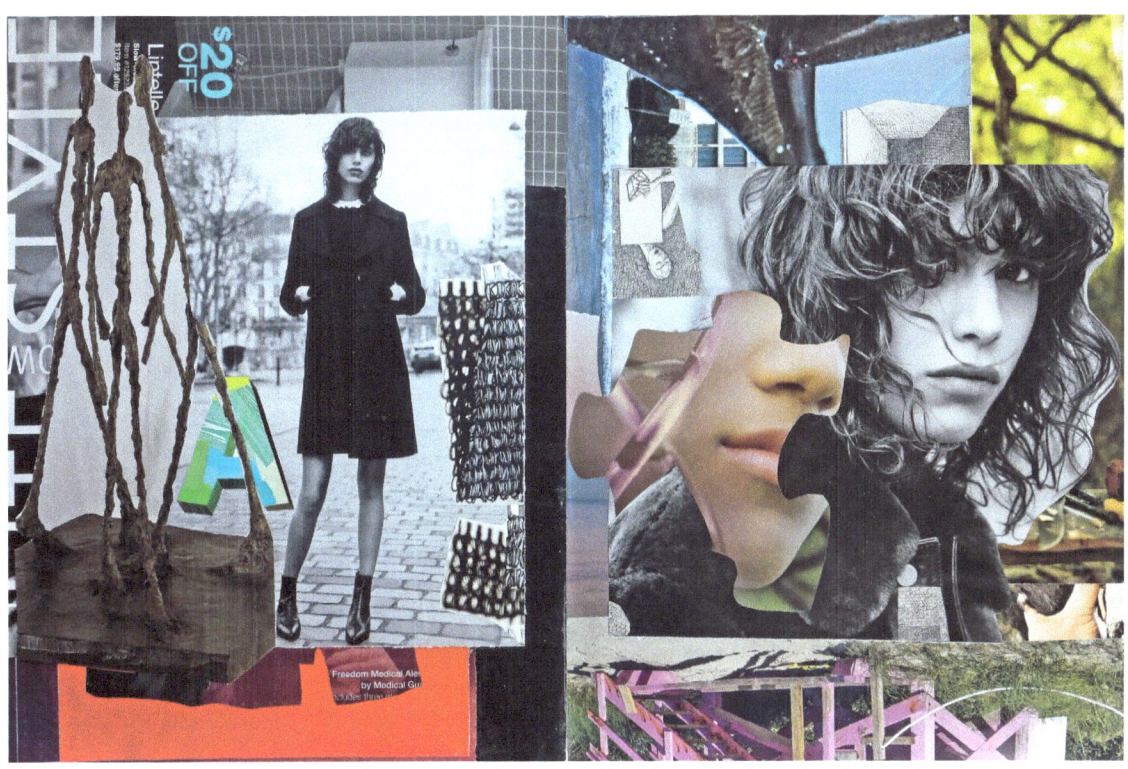

Using an Old Book as a Gluebook

The idea of taking an old, unloved, out of date book, and breathing new life into it with artwork is near and dear to my heart. Many gluebookers end up using old books at some point, because they offer a more substantial surface to glue upon than comp books or cheap lined journals.

Old books need a little bit of prep work before they're used for artwork. Here's a peek at my old thesaurus gluebook, which is a work in progress:

Start with a book that's in good shape. Make sure the covers aren't hanging too loose, and that the pages are well stitched, rather than glued to the spine. A book can be old and unloved without being ready to fall apart!

When purchasing a book to use, consider the size and number of pages. This book has a lot of pages, so I've been working in it off and on for years.

This is called a stub. It's what is left behind when you remove pages from a book, to reduce the stress on the spine caused by adding in the bulk of layers of glued pieces. Never tear out pages all the way down to the spine, because it can weaken the book, causing it to fall apart.

Removing pages also helps keep the book from splaying out in a wedge shape when it's full.

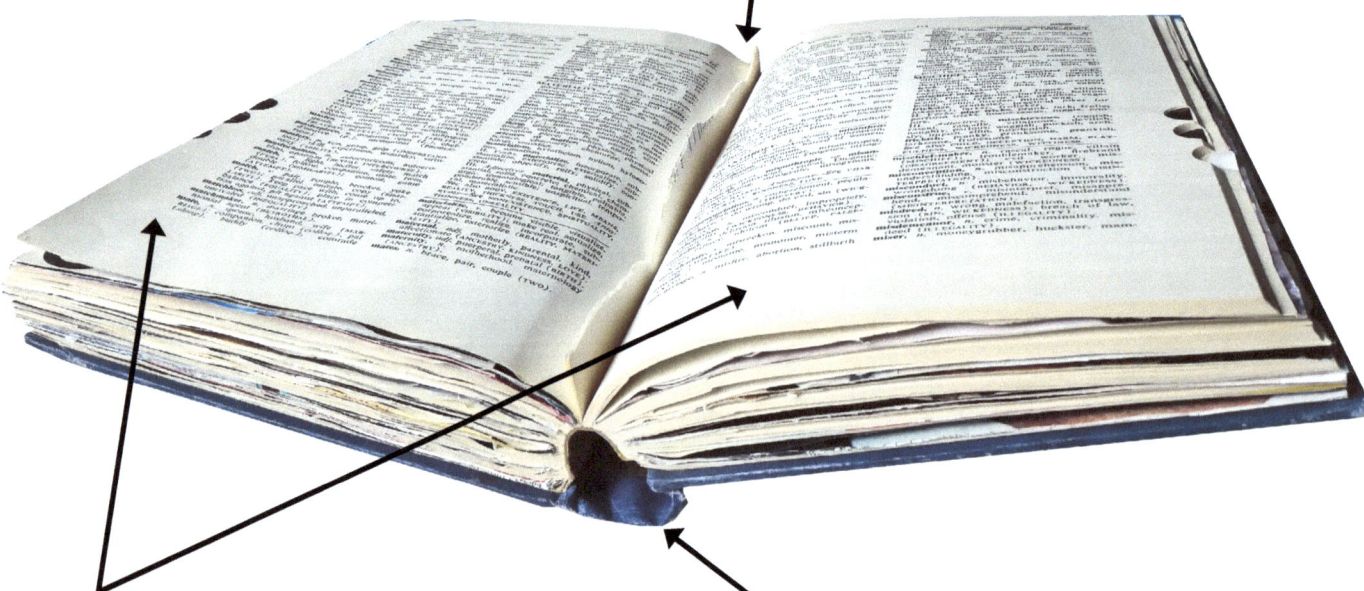

See the blank pages on either side of the stub? I'm going to apply glue to both pages, and the stub, and press them together. That hides the stub, and creates a strong page for me to work upon.

See this space between the cover and the spine? That's a good thing. That means the pages are stitched, rather than glued. You always want to work in a book that's stitched. Glued page blocks will fall apart spectacularly under pressure. Don't use a glued book!

Gluebook Challenges

Some artists find challenges provide the motivation to create more regularly. When combined with gluebooking, these challenges can be a quick, effective way to make room for art in a busy day.

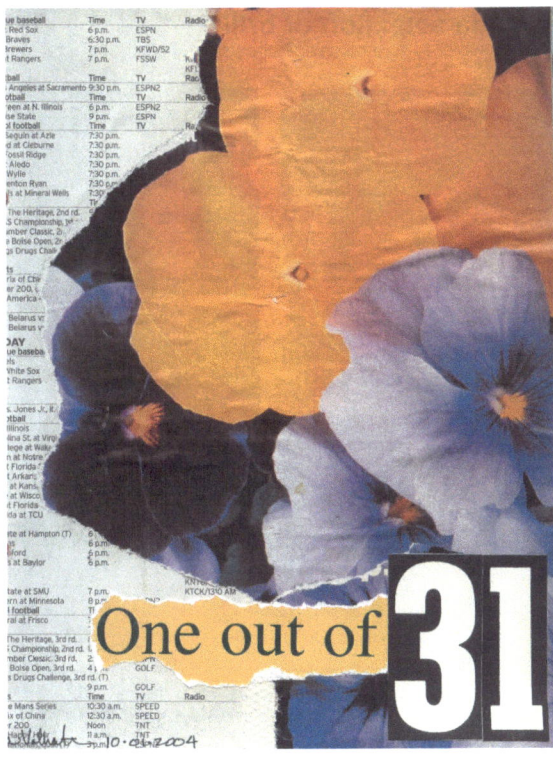

Page a Day Challenge

One of the simplest challenges is to create a page every day for a specific amount of time. The gluebook pages shown here are from a daily challenge during the month of October, and I created 31 pages in 31 days.

Committing to make one page a day for a week, or a month, is a great way to make creating a daily habit, rather than something that constantly gets pushed to the bottom of the list.

A little later, I'll show you my work from a daily gluecard challenge I organized right before I started writing this book. Even after many years of gluebooking, I still find daily challenges helpful to clear away the cobwebs.

One Magazine Challenge

Here's a challenge you can pick up and do any time: grab one magazine, and make as many gluebook pages as you can, using only what you find in that magazine.

I recently did a sort of expanded version of this challenge, while I was working on some Kickstarter reward books. I pulled half a dozen magazines into a pile, and made as many gluebook pages as I could from those. I pretty much filled 20 sets of gluebook pages from that one small pile of magazines.

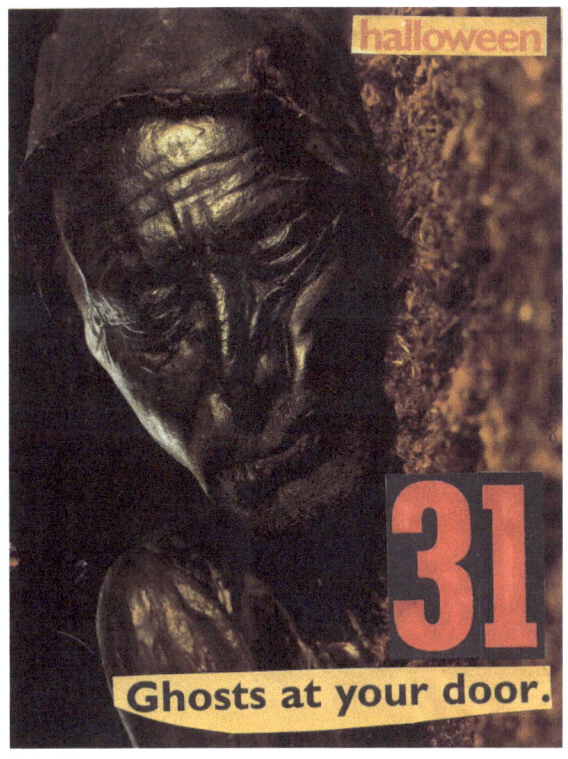

Gluebook Pages by Jaleen Brooks

Colorado Springs, Colorado

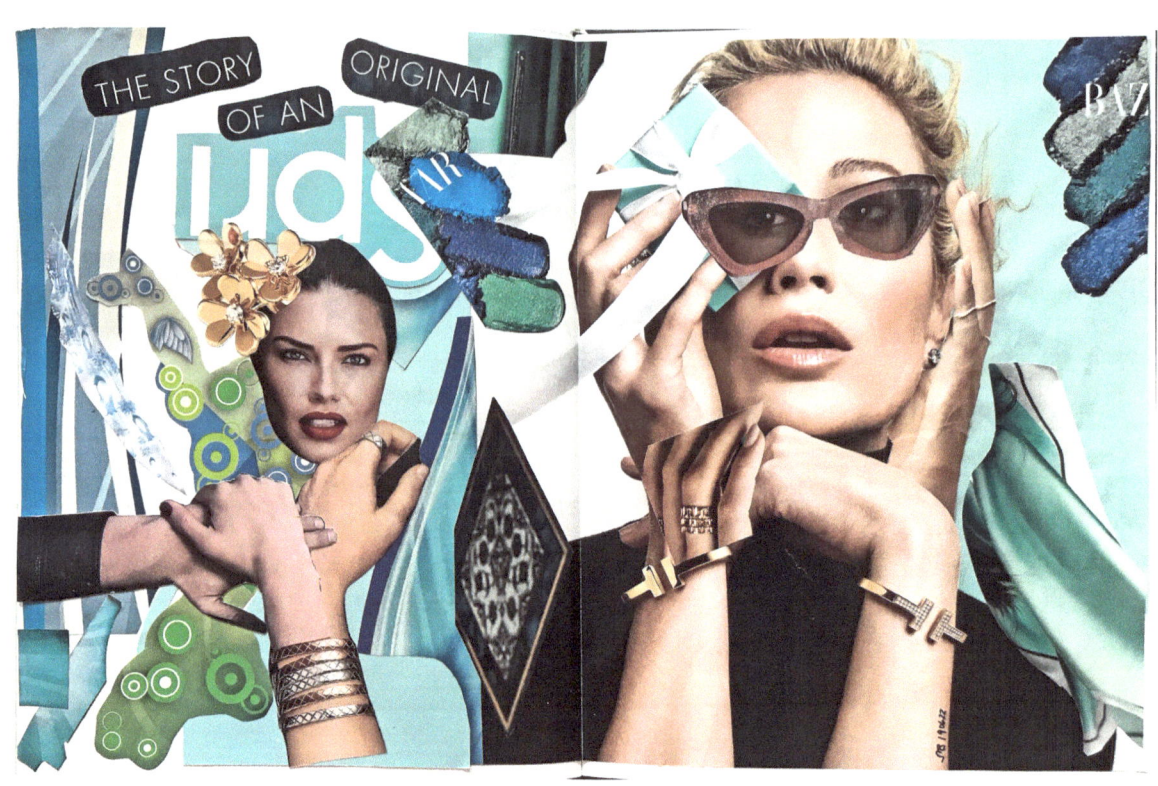

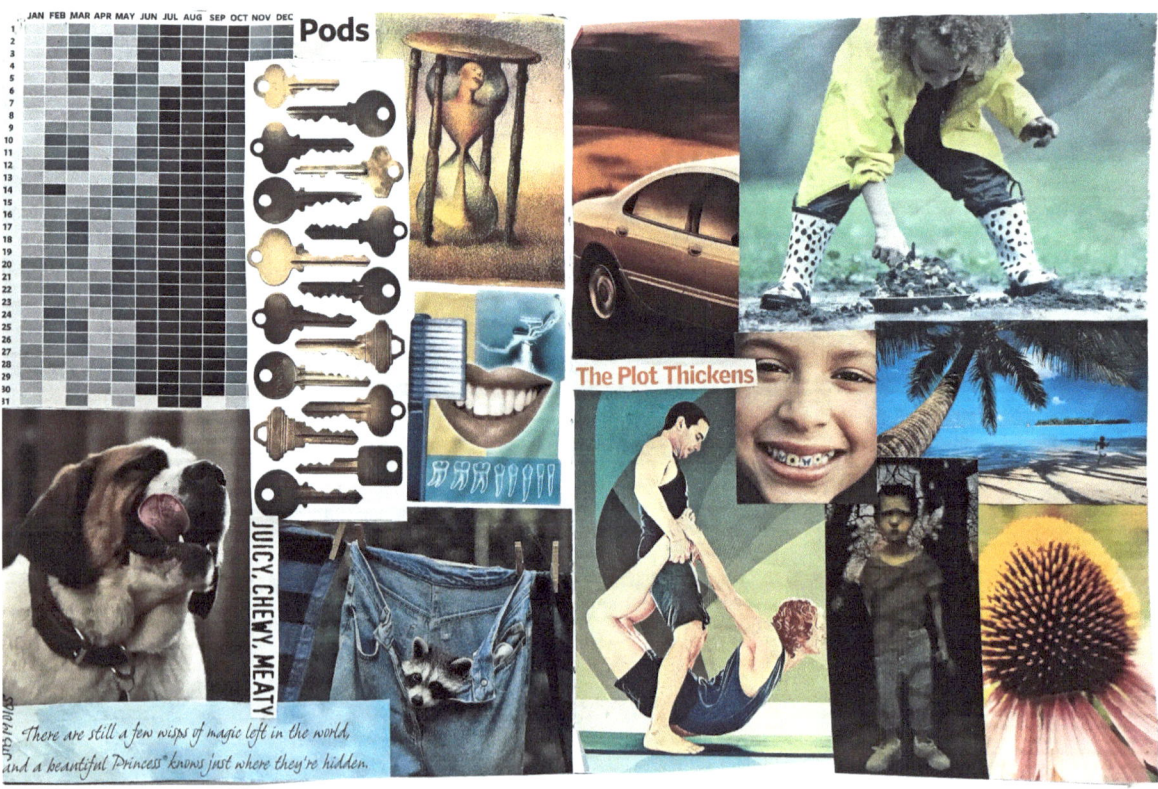

"It's very cathartic for me to cut up images and glue them into different designs. What will I get?"

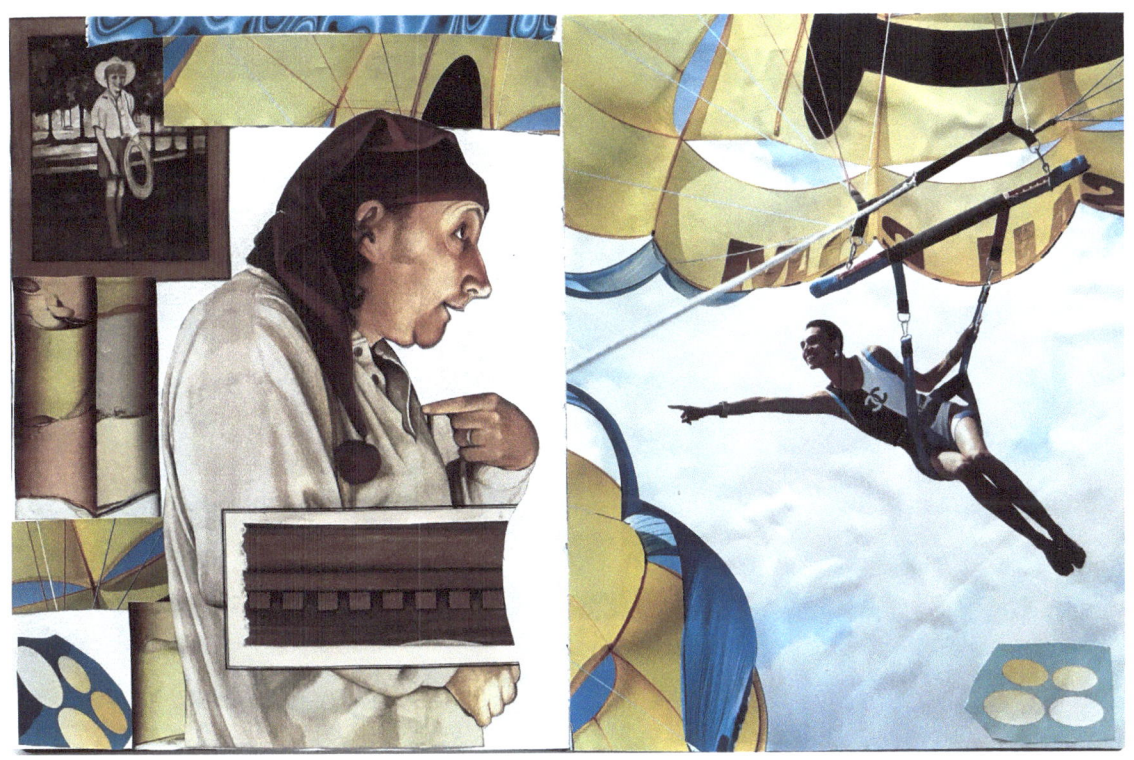

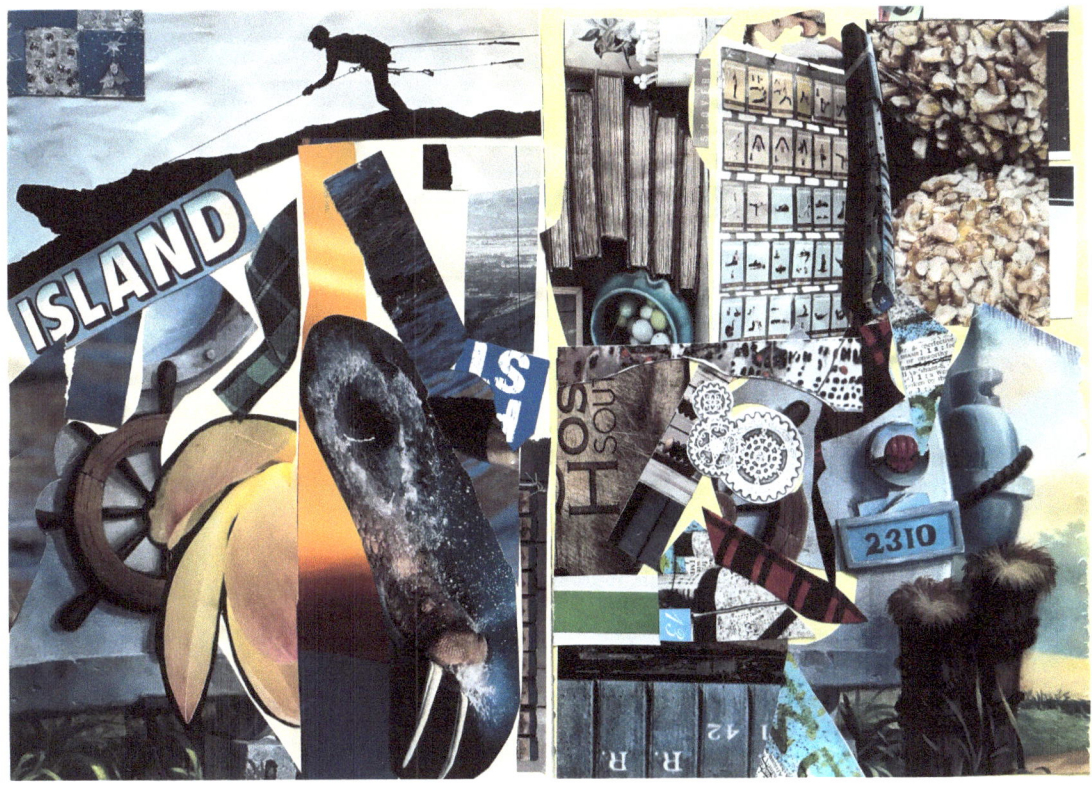

How To Make an Easy Junk Journal

A junk journal is just what is sounds like: a journal made from junk mail. Taking the idea of using what you have one step further, and making your gluebook from things you've rescued from the recycle bin is a lot of fun, and makes for a completely handmade finished book.

To make an easy junk journal, you'll need:

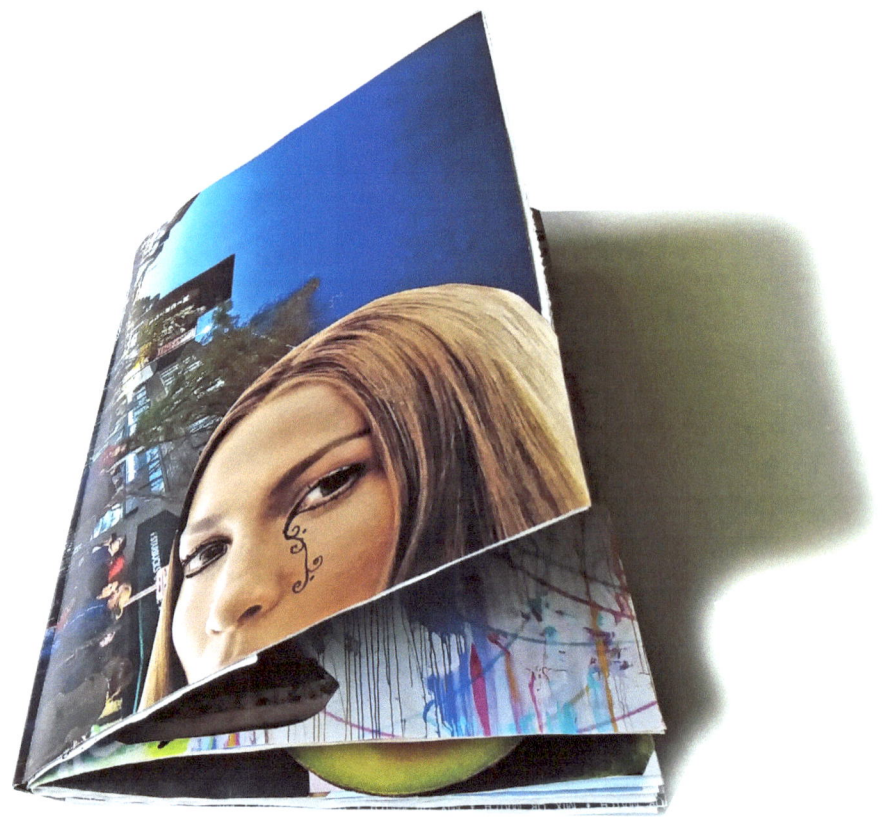

- Junk mail. I like to use the clump of fliers that come once a week, with multi-page ads printed on newsprint. Save the heavier sheets with pre-punched coupons to use as covers. You can also make this type of journal from magazine or catalog pages.

- An L-square. If you don't care whether your pages are perfectly square, a ruler will do.

- A craft knife with fresh blades. Don't cut with dull blades. I have a scar on my index finger to explain why.

- An awl. If you make a lot of books, an awl is a useful hole-punching tool. If not, a big needle will work in a pinch.

- A piece of scrap cardboard, to back up your pages when punching.

- Waxed linen thread. Linen thread is sold in craft stores for jewelry making, and wherever book binding supplies are sold. In a pinch, cotton thread and a block of beeswax will work. Do not sew paper by hand using polyester thread, because it will rip right through.

- A glue stick, or your favorite dry glue. I really prefer not to use wet glues on lightweight papers.

- A brayer, to make sure whatever is glued gets good contact, and stays flat.

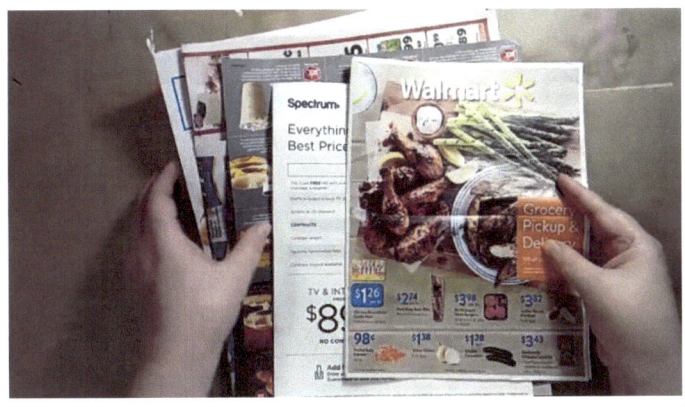

1. Sort through your pile of junk mail, and find a multi-page ad, or several pieces that are about the size you want to work with.

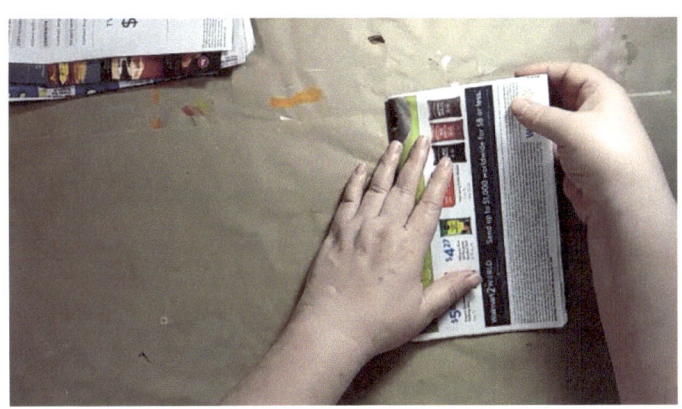

2. Fold the ad in half.

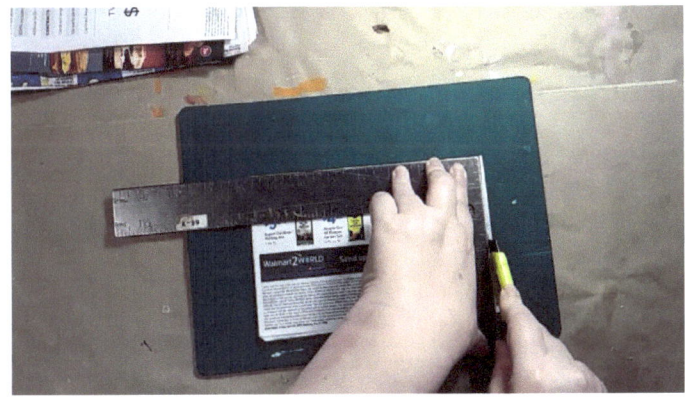

3. Using an L-square and a craft knife, trim off the top fold, to create indvidual pages.

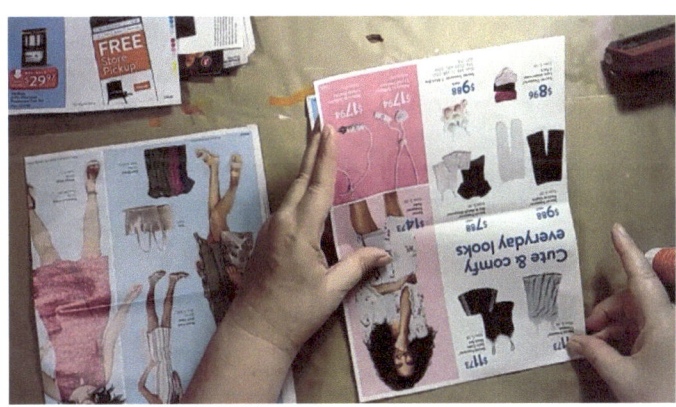

4. If your paper is very thin, you might want to glue two together, back to back, to give yourself a stronger surface to work on. Glue with a glue stick. line the pages up, and use a brayer to make them good and flat.

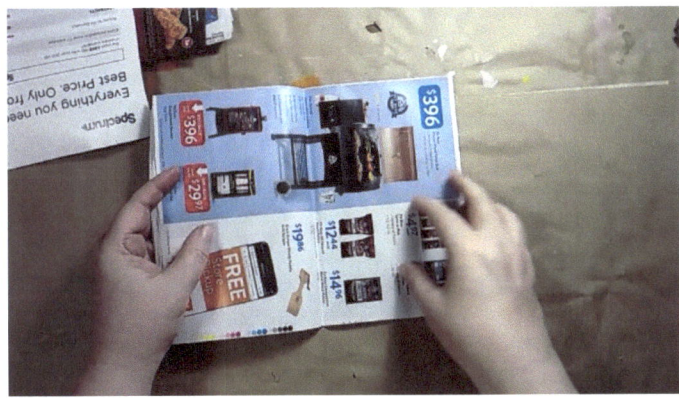

5. Stack your folded pages together, lining them up at the top, bottom, and fold.

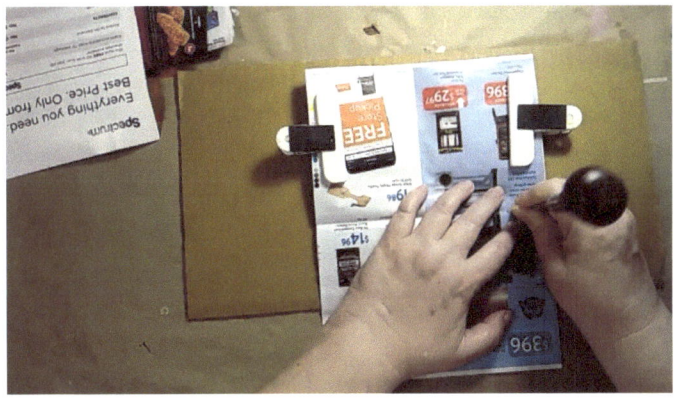

6. Clamp the pages together, and make a set of evenly spaced marks along the fold. I made mine about 1" apart. Place the pages on a piece of cardboard, and use an awl to punch holes through all the layers at the marks.

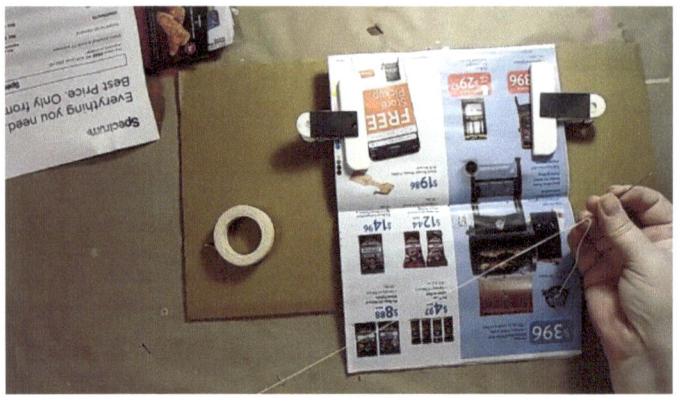

7. Thread a needle with waxed linen thread. Cut the thread so it's double the length of the spine of your journal, plus a foot extra.

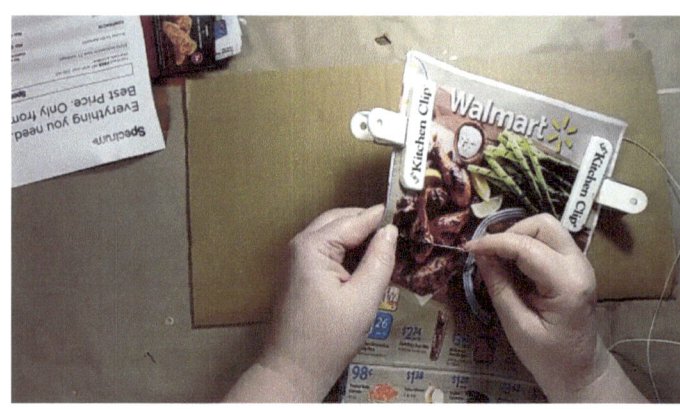

8. Flip the book over, and push the needle down the second hole from the top of the spine.

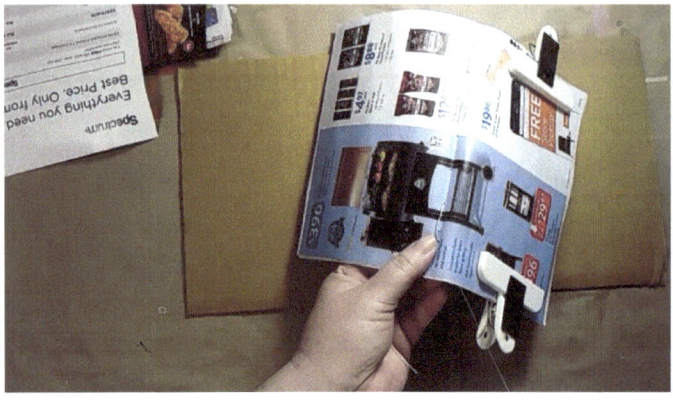

9. Flip the book back to the inside, and pull the thread through, leaving a long tail. Push the needle through the first hole, and pull the thread taut, to make your first stitch on the inside of the spine.

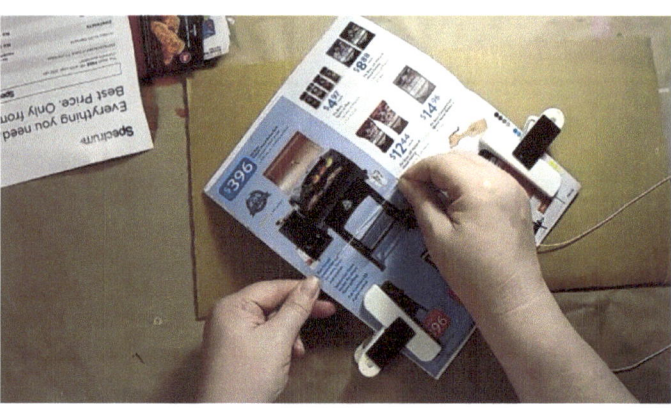

10. Now, push the needle back up through the second hole, being careful not to stitch through the thread that's already there. This will lock your first stitch and the tail in place.

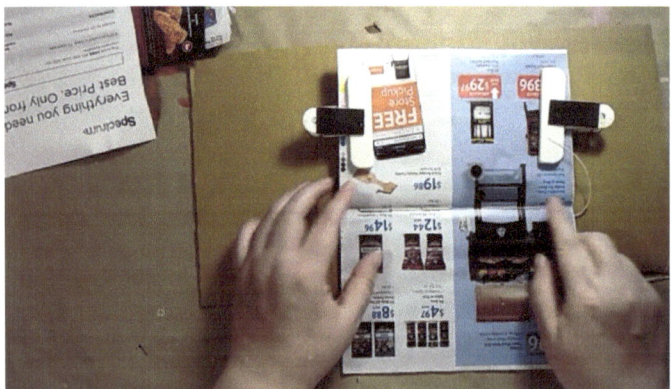

11. Do a running stitch, up and down, through the holes, to the end of the spine.

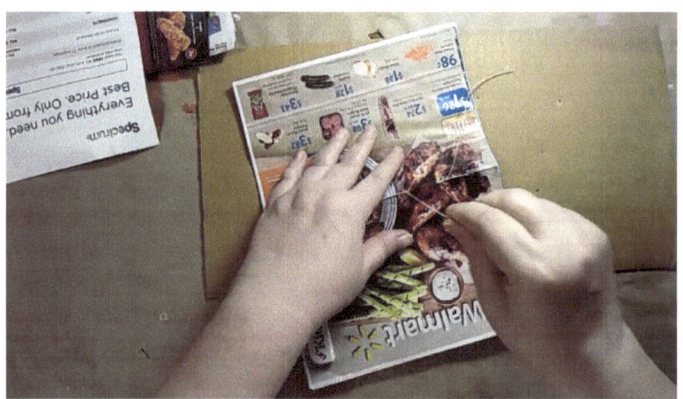

12. Bring your thread back up through the second hole from the bottom, and do a running stitch back up to the third hole from the top. This should leave you on the outside of the spine, with an empty space, not filled with thread.

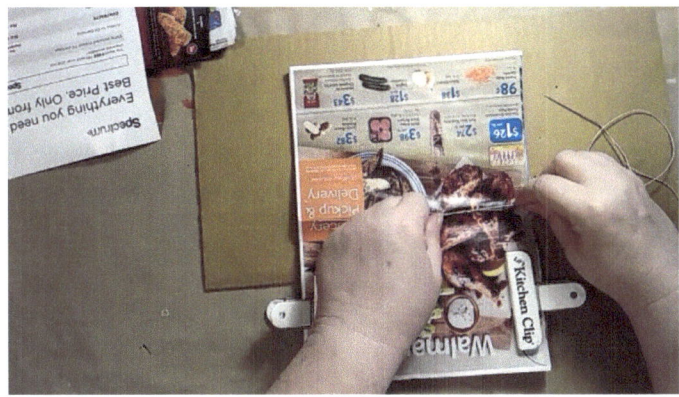

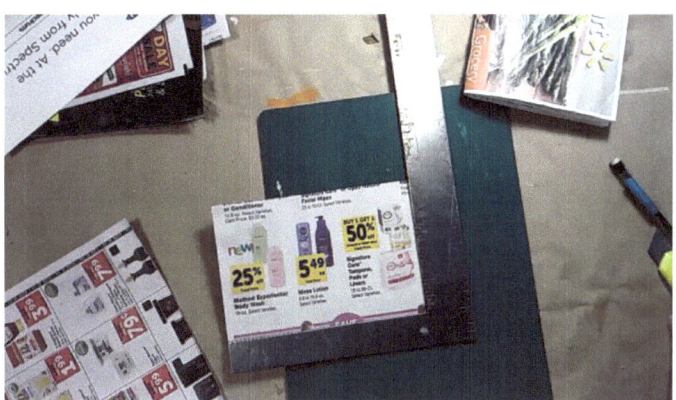

13. Wrap the two tails around each other several times, pulling them taut. The wax and the tension will create a tight hold, and you'll have a nice, flat finish to your stitching. Trim the tails away.

14. Cut a cover that's slightly taller and wider than your pages from another piece of junk mail. A heavy ad with coupons might only need one layer, while a lightweight one might require two.

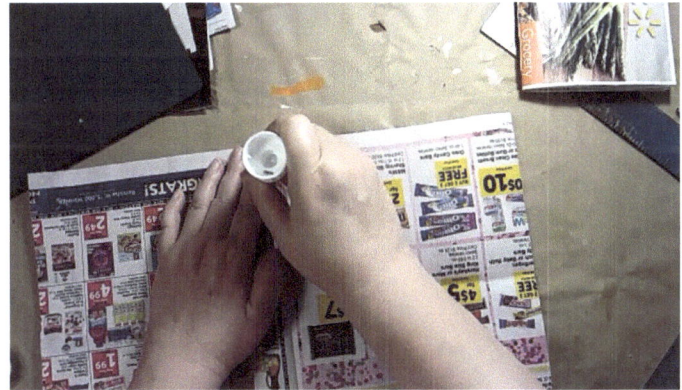

15. Glue your cover layers together if necessary.

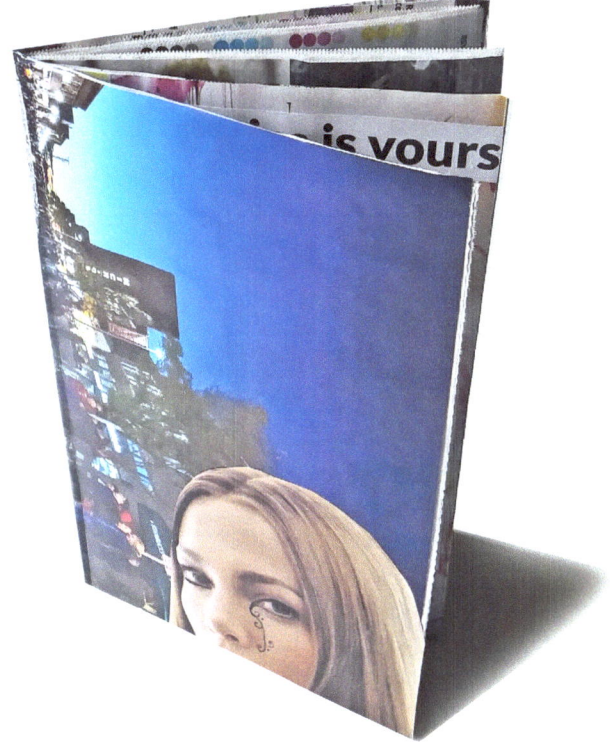

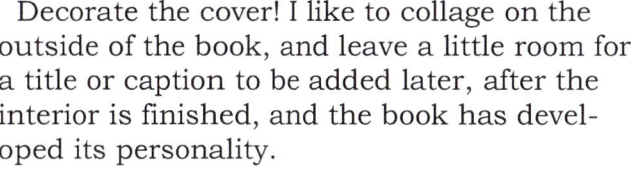

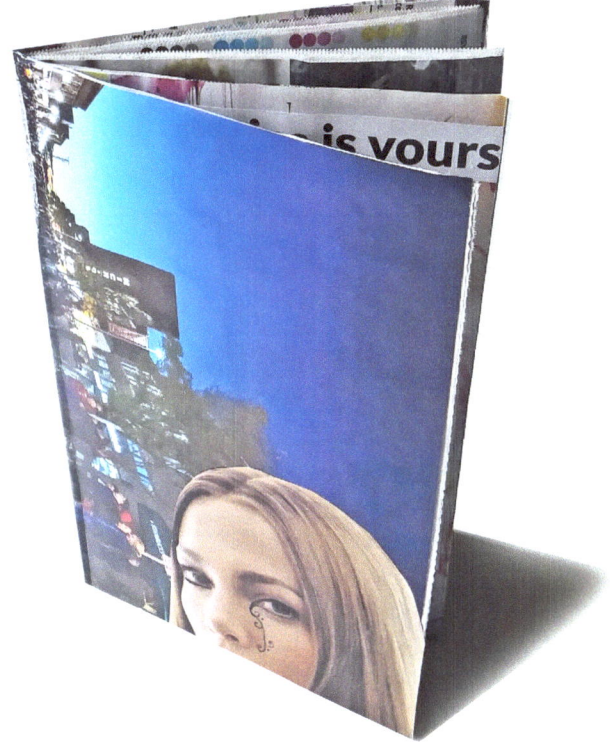

16. Apply glue to the front page of your journal, and press it onto the inside front cover, lining up the folds. Do the same for the back page and back cover.

Decorate the cover! I like to collage on the outside of the book, and leave a little room for a title or caption to be added later, after the interior is finished, and the book has developed its personality.

Gluebook Pages by Corinne Stubson

Medford, Oregon

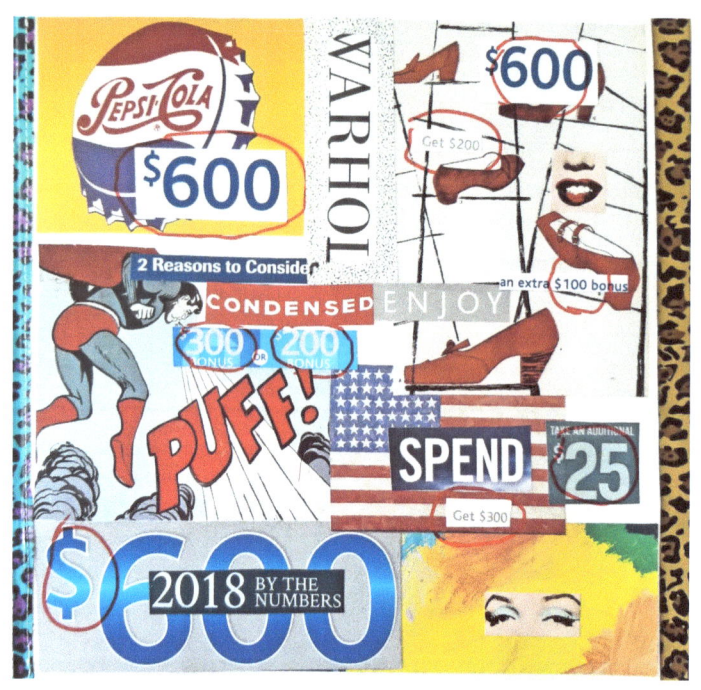

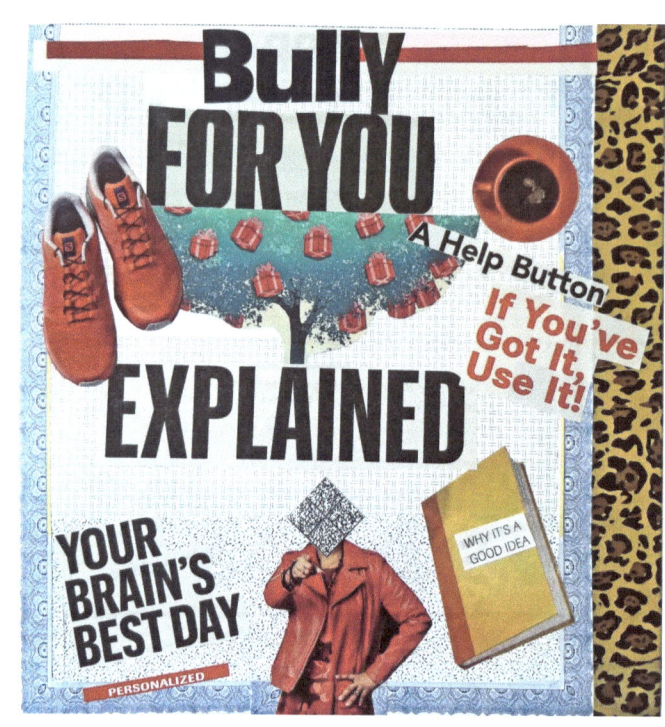

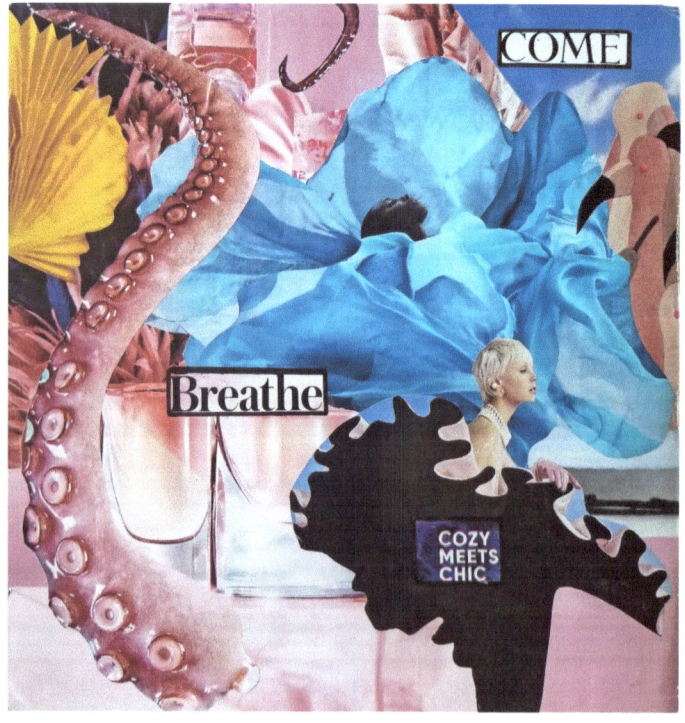

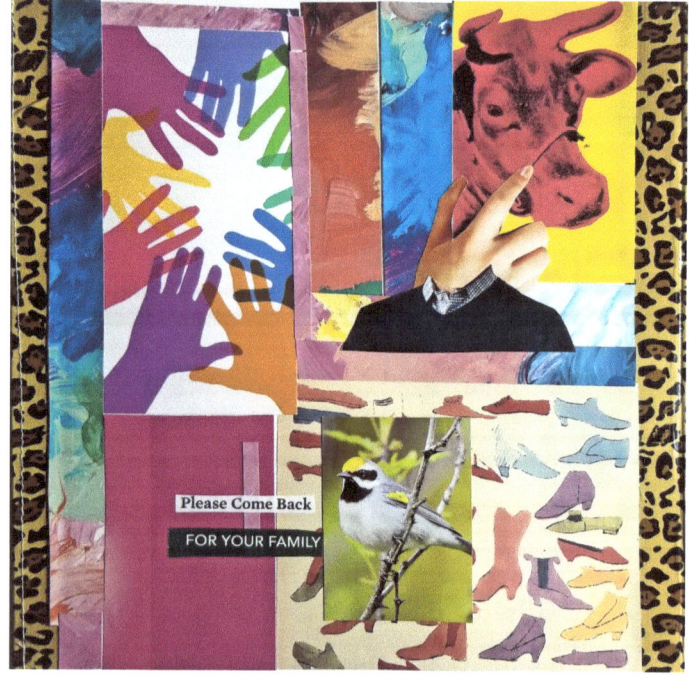

"I discovered gluebooks through the Yahoo altered books group around 2005 or 2006."

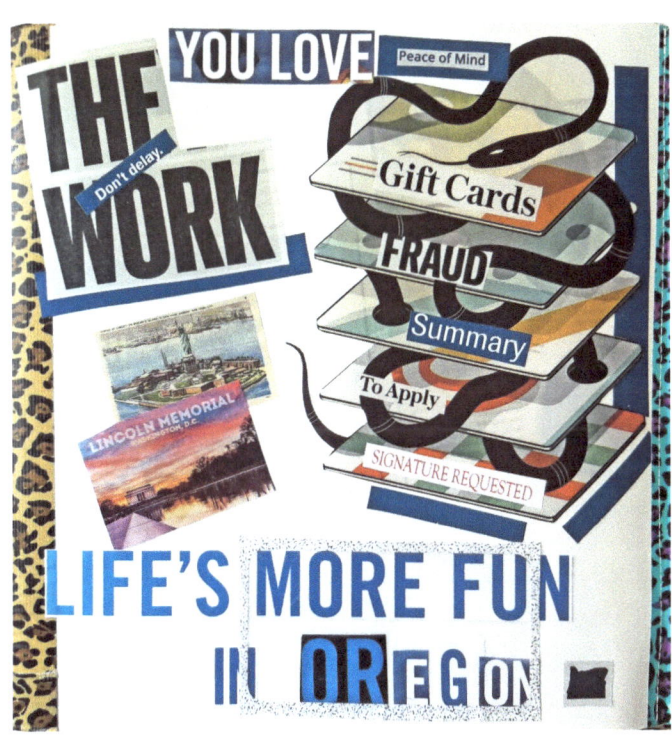

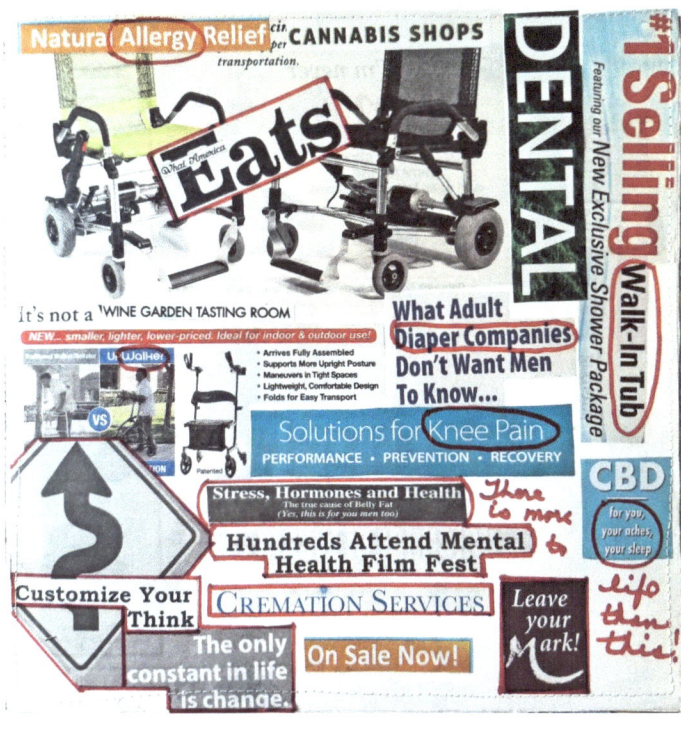

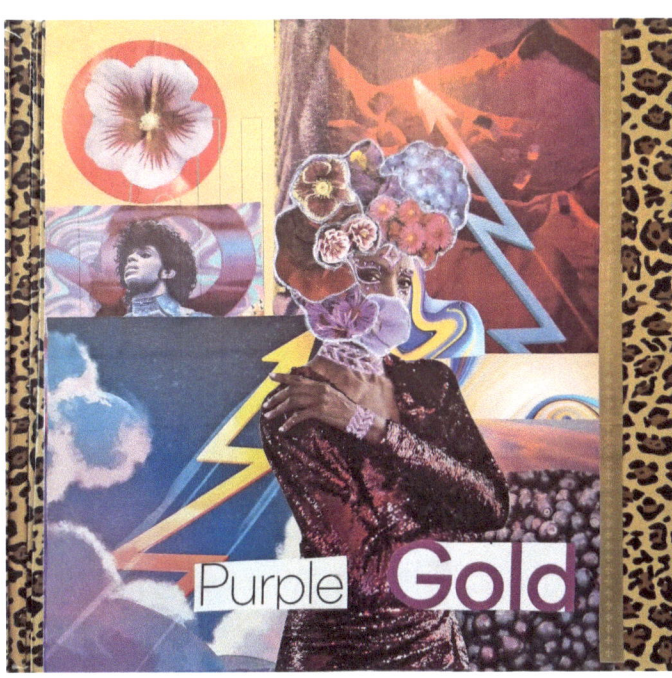

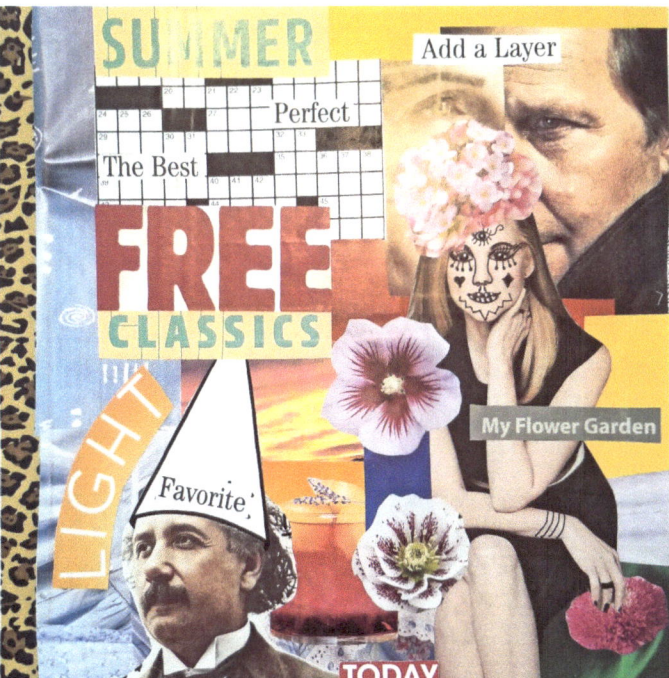

What is a Gluecard?

In the same way that a gluebook is a book that contains glued work, a gluecard is a card with glued work on the front.

I've organized gluecard swaps, where the cards are made postcard sized (4x6), with blank backs, like glued postcards. I've seen people do variations of the Index Card a Day (ICAD) challenge, using various sizes of index cards, as their bases. Really, any card-type base can be used to create a gluecard.

These are a handful of gluecards I've made for swaps:

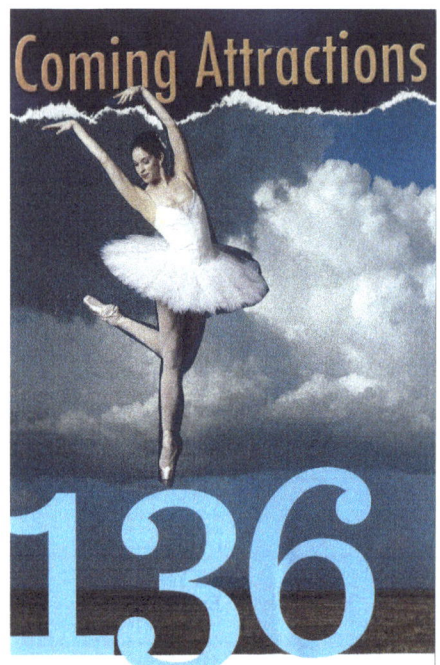
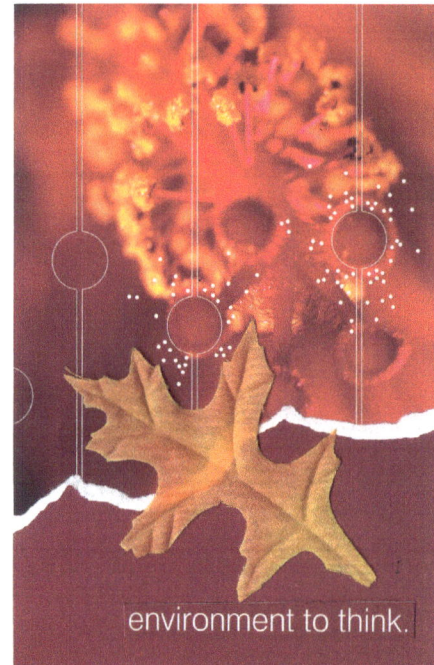
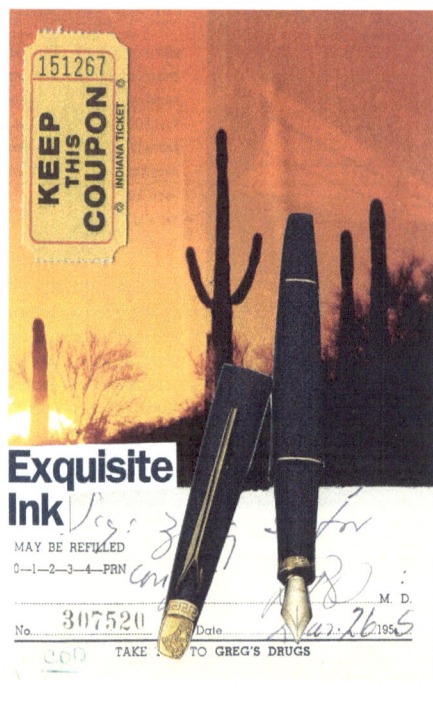
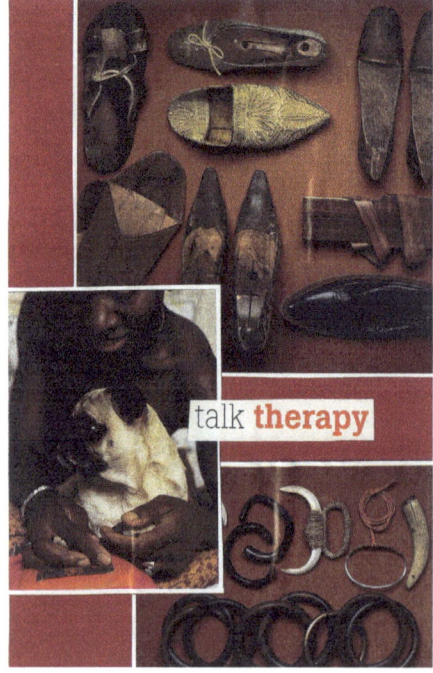
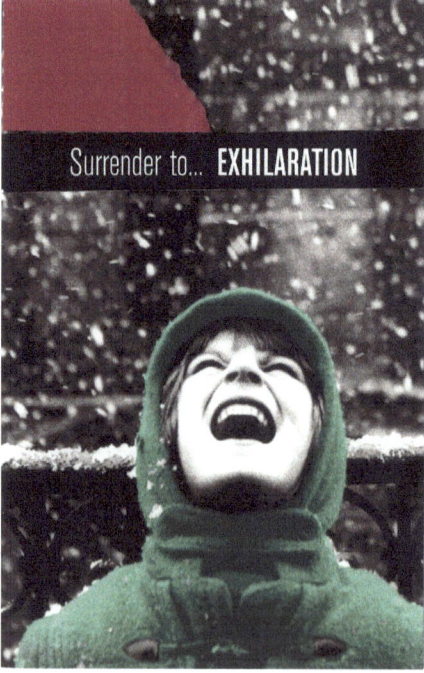
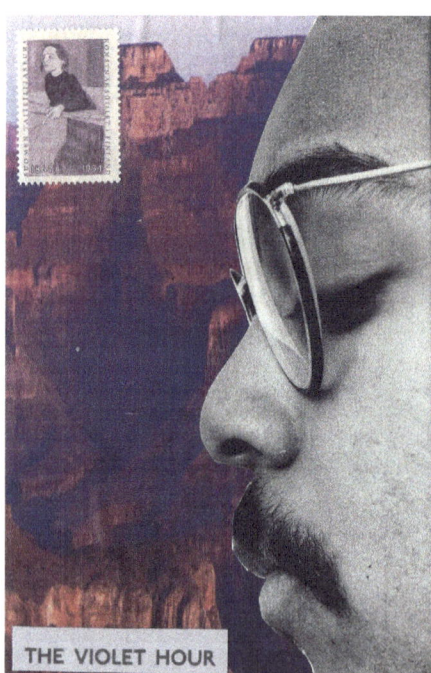

How to Make a Simple Gluecard

To make a gluecard, all you need is a magazine, a 4x6 inch index card, scissors, and a glue stick, or your glue of choice.

1. Start with a background.

I like to use large textural images, and cut them down. Apply glue to an index card, position on the back of the image, and use a brayer to get it flat. Trim around the edges.

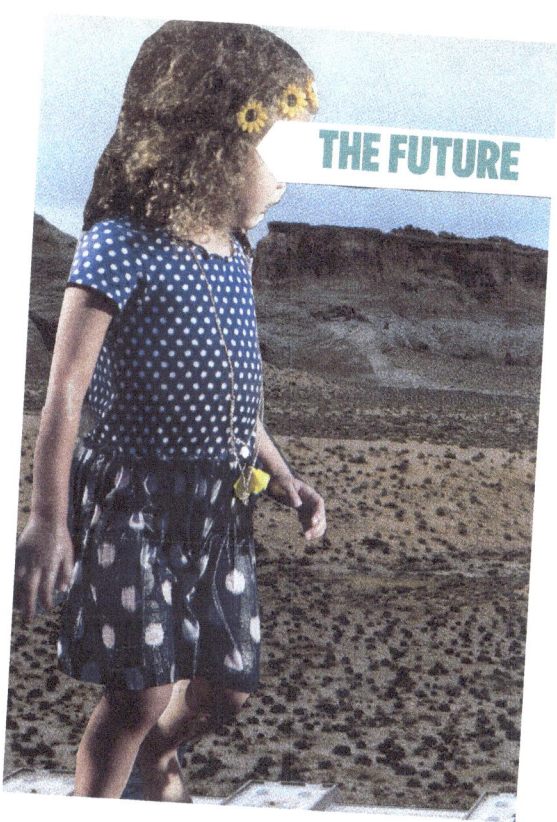

THE FUTURE

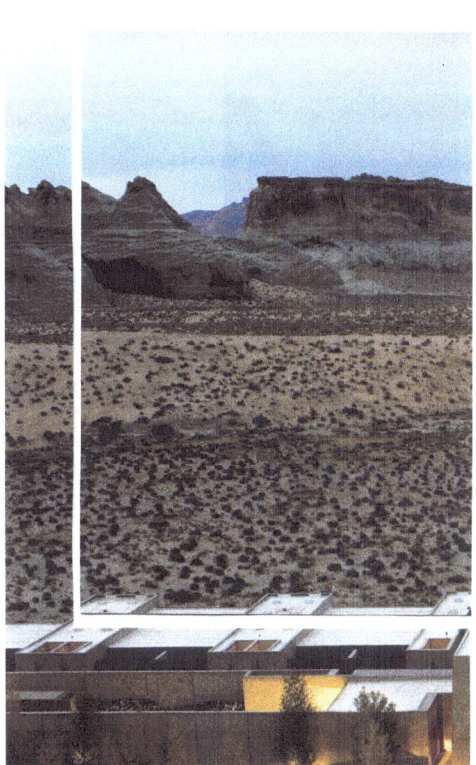

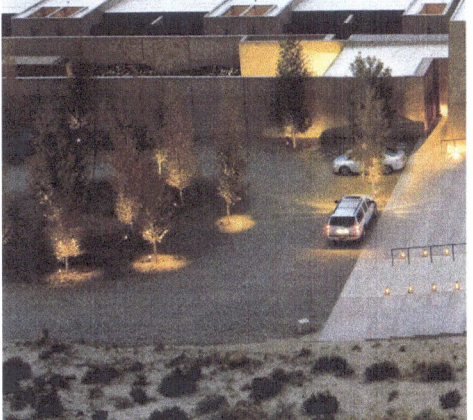

2. Add an image.

Pick something that takes up at least a third of the background space. I like to hang my main image over the top, bottom and side of the card. Do some fussy cutting with sharp scissors to get all the details, and apply with glue and a brayer.

CITY OF
THE FUTURE

3. Find a good caption.

Add a word or two that suits your story. I like to pick the words last, after the background and image are glued down. A little swipe of glue, and you're done!

Gluecard a Day Challenge (GCAD)

I came up with doing a gluecard a day as a challenge for the gluebooks group on Facebook. Every day for a month, I posted a prompt, and participants were free to use it or not, to create a gluecard, using whatever base they chose. It was sort of a variation of the popular index card a day challenge (ICAD), minus the techniques and products.

This sort of small, daily creation challenge is good for getting into the habit of making a little time for art every day. Doing it with gluecards simplifies that, by eliminating the need for any supplies beyond some index cards, a glue stick, and a pile of magazines.

Here are the cards I made for the first year of the challenge, with the prompts for each day:

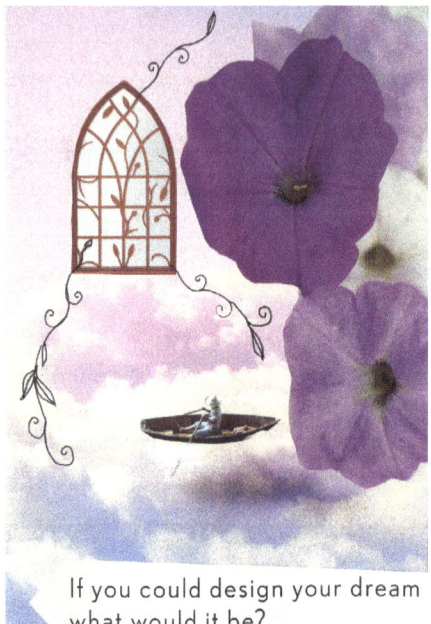

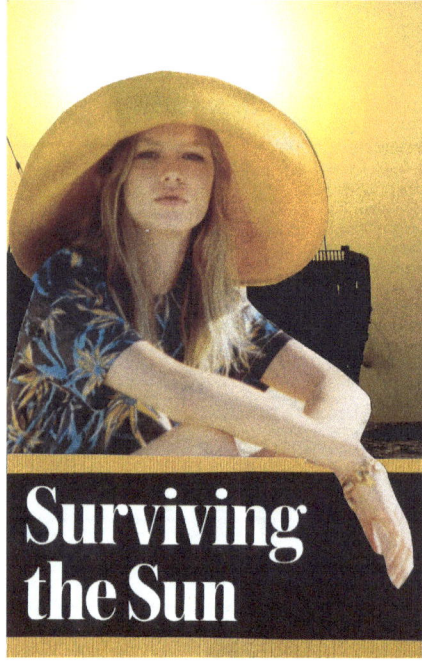

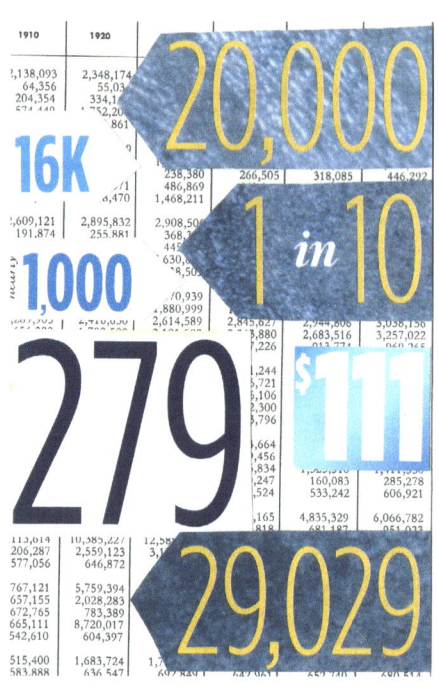

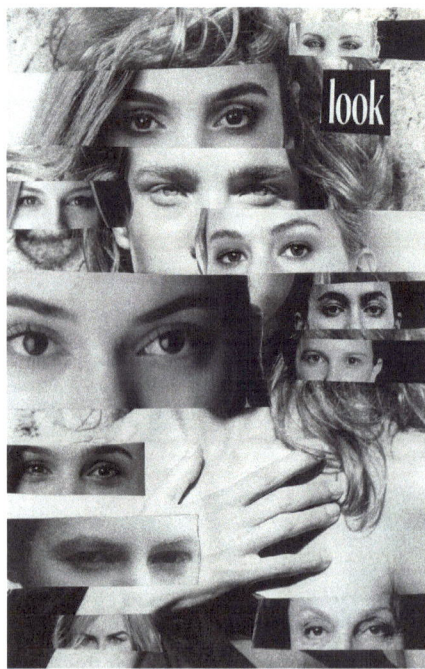

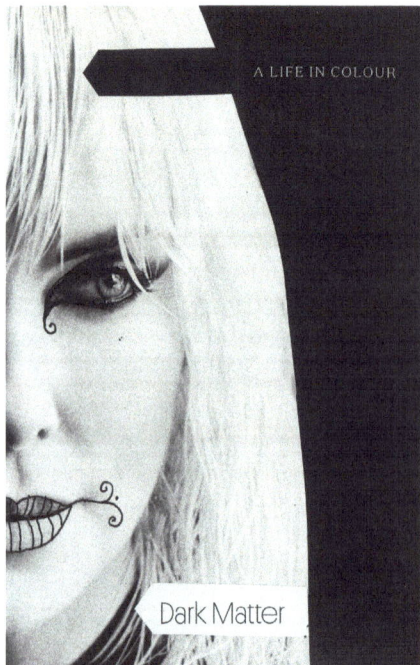

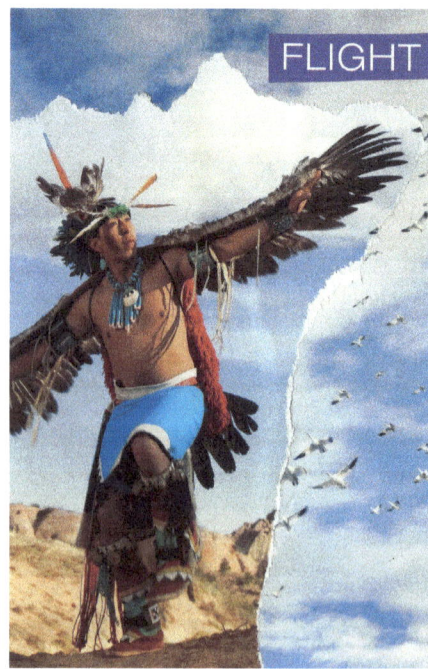

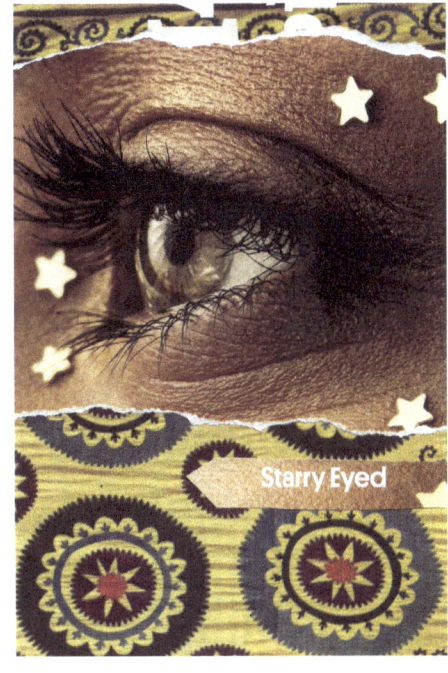

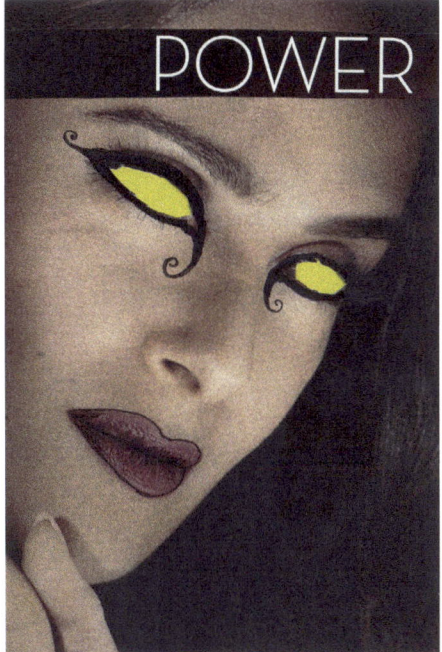

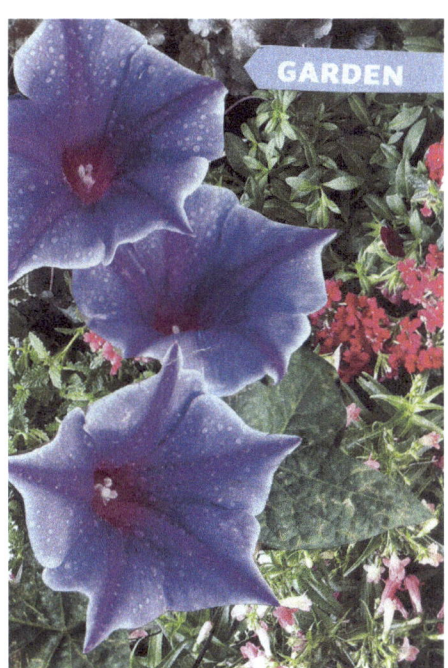

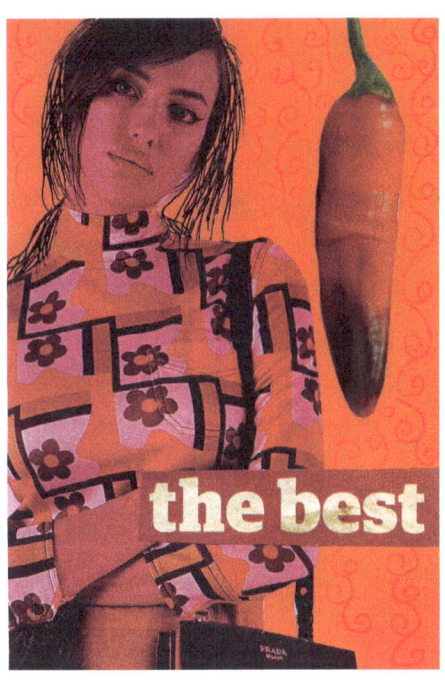

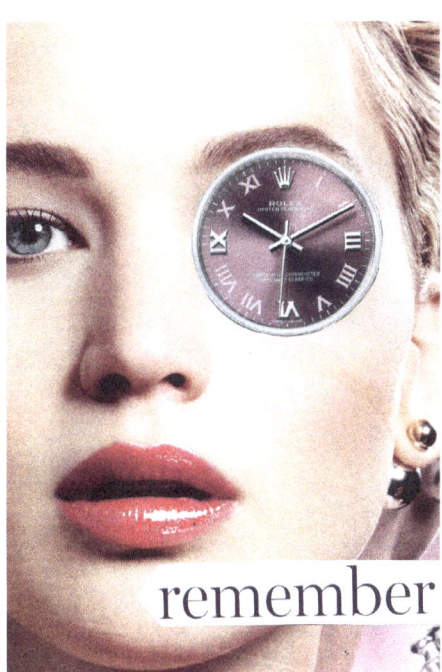

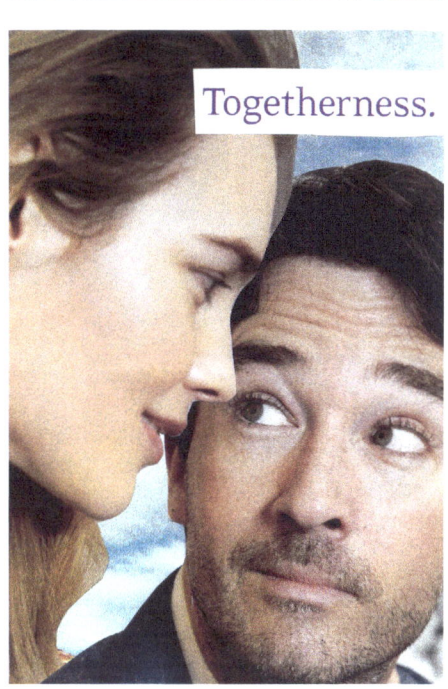

Opposite page:

1. Dream 2. Sun 3. Numbers

4. Eyes 5. Black & 6. Wings
white

This page:

7. Stars 8. Evil 9. Flowers

10. Red 11. Time 12. Love

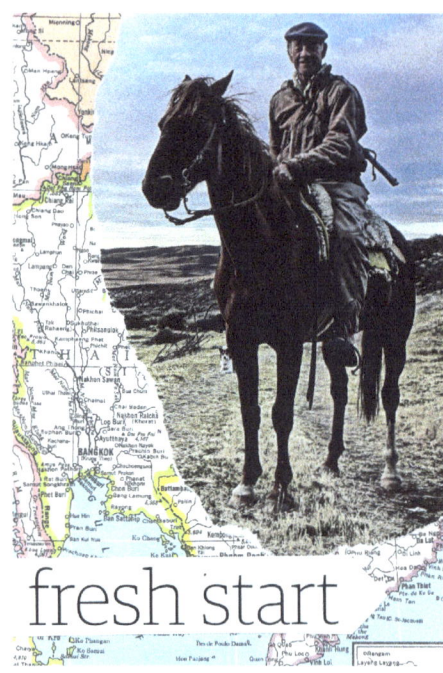

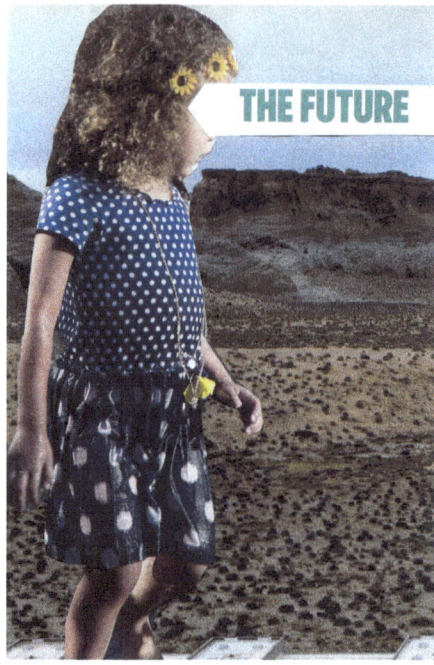

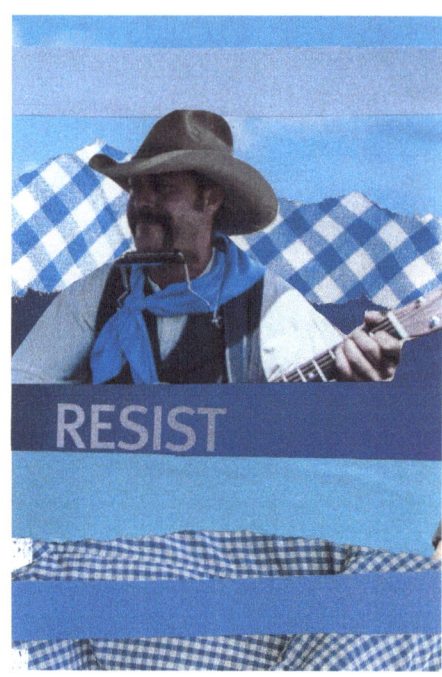

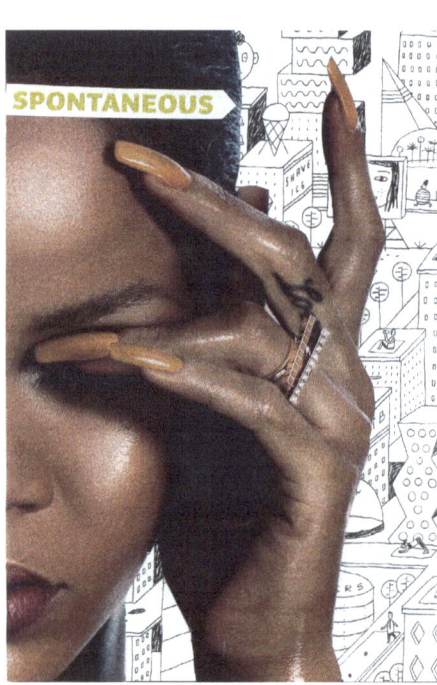

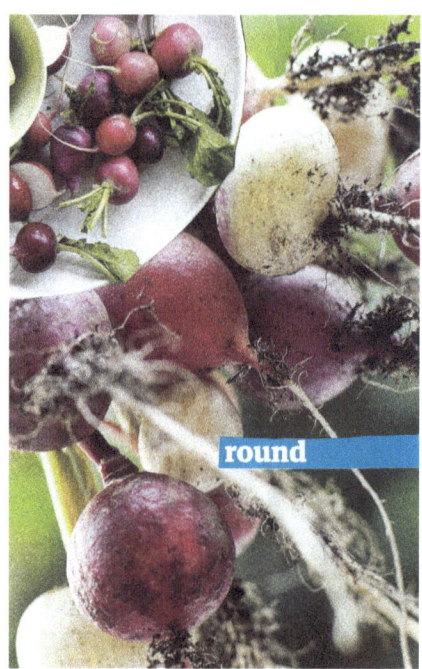

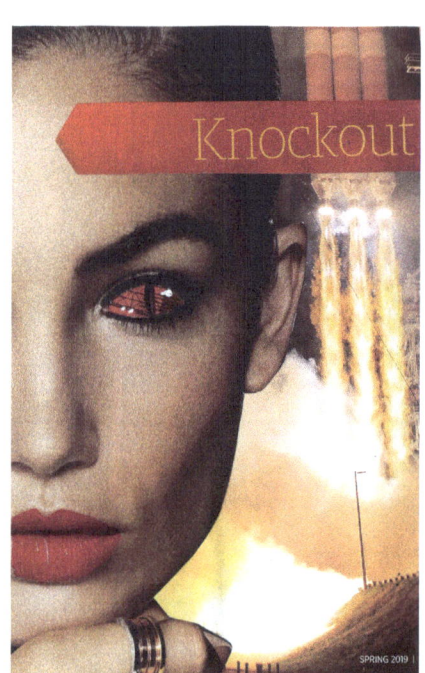

Working With Prompts

I offered the participants in the GCAD project a list of daily prompts, to use as the inspiration for their gluecards. Prompts come in many forms; they can be words or phrases, colors, or even techniques or suggestions to use specific media.

Prompts are suggestions. They're meant to act as sparks for that day's creation. Some days, a prompt will immediately light the creative fire. Other days, they will lead me down a trail that's far from where I started. Some days? Nothing. That's OK. Prompts should be something that are helpful, rather than a hindrance. On days when the prompt doesn't do anything for me, the solution is to just make whatever comes out, rather than trying to force something, or not create at all.

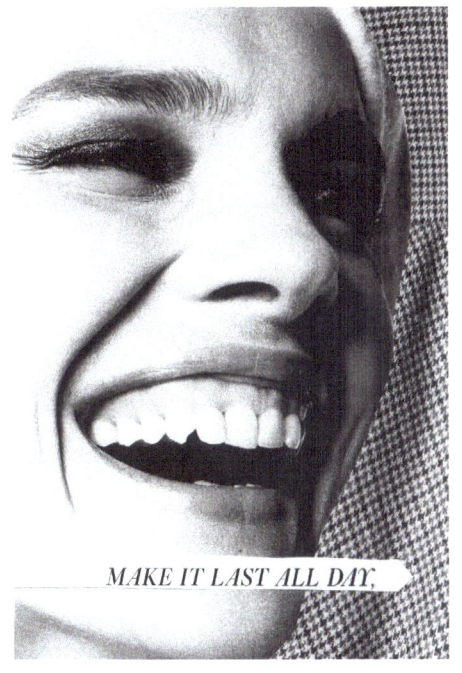

MAKE IT LAST ALL DAY,

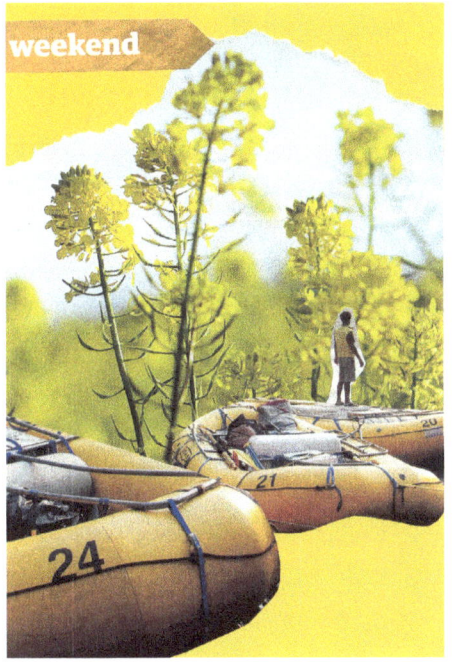

weekend

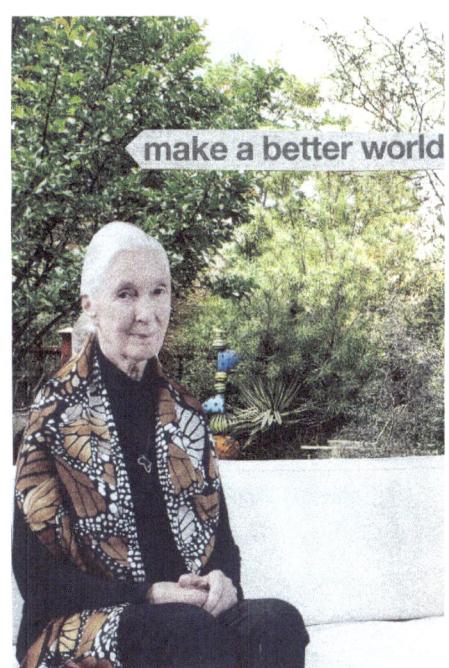

make a better world

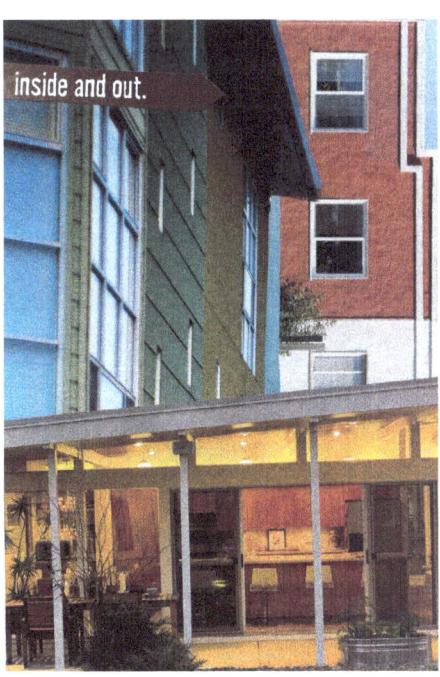

inside and out.

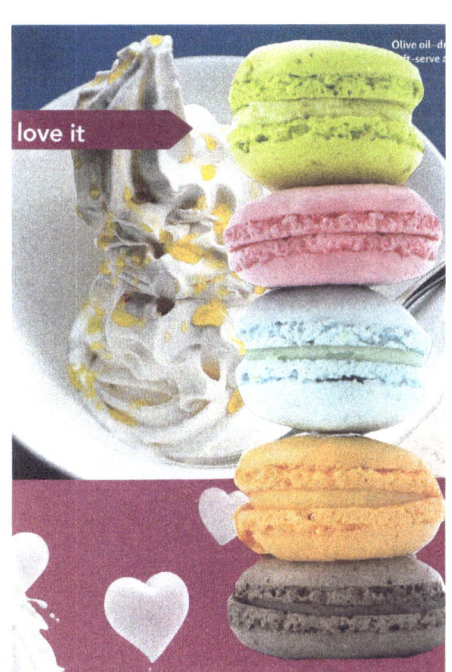

love it

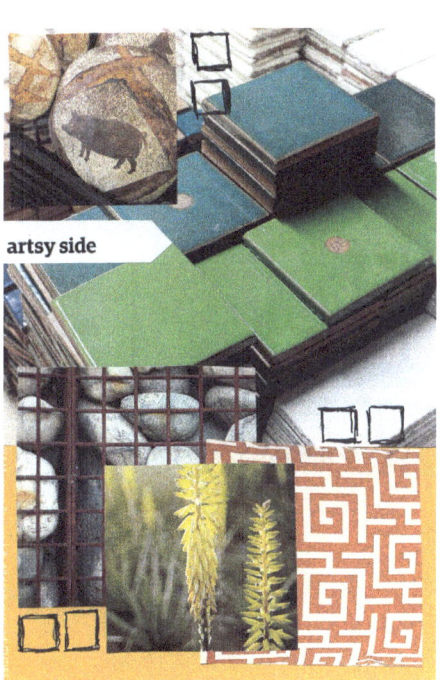

artsy side

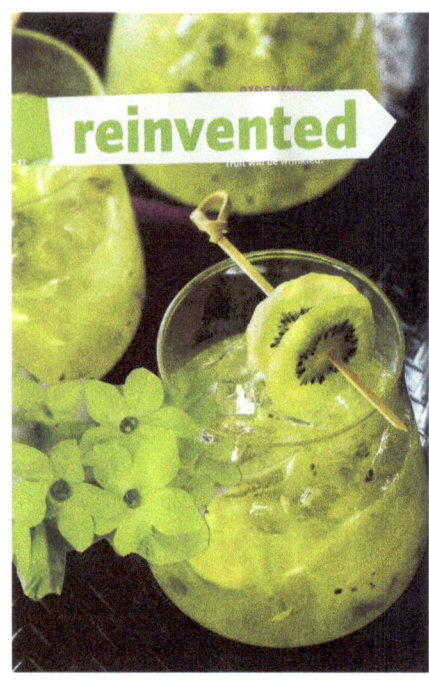

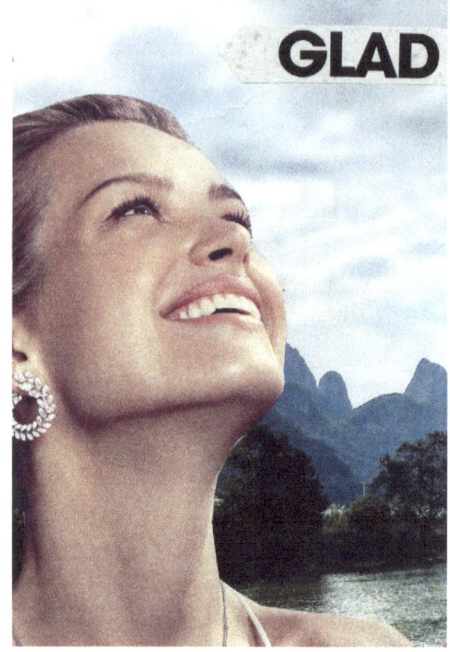

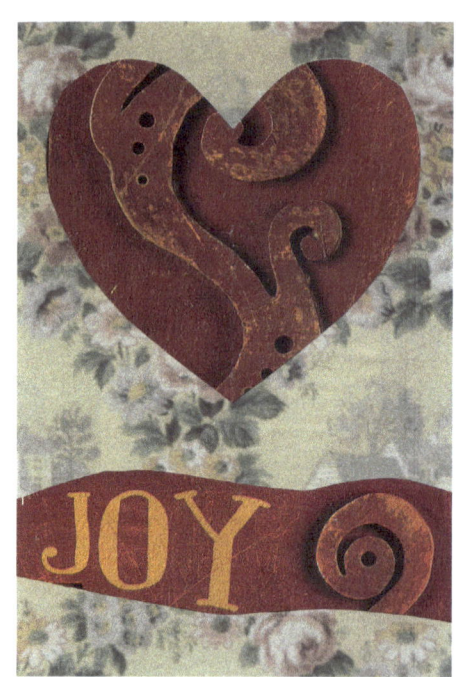

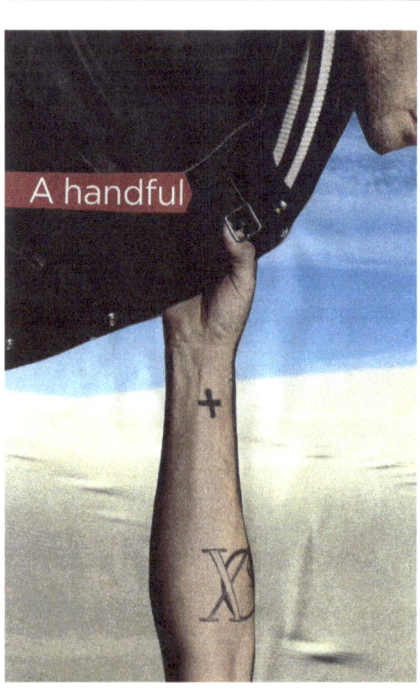

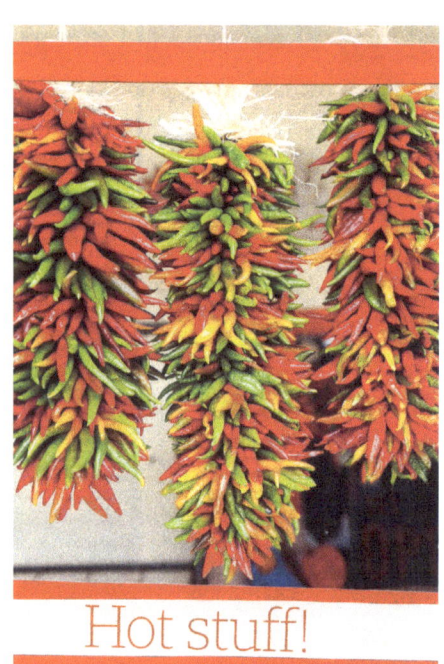

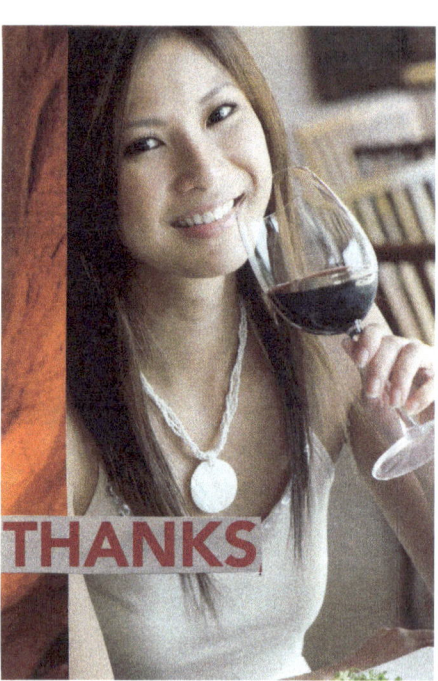

25. Green   26. Joy   27. Heart

28. Reach   29. Hot   30. Thanks

Gluecard Swap Gallery

I've hosted quite a few gluecard swaps over the years. Gluecards offer a no stress, no supplies required entry to swapping art that many artists find appealing.

These are cards from one the most recent gluecard swaps I've hosted.

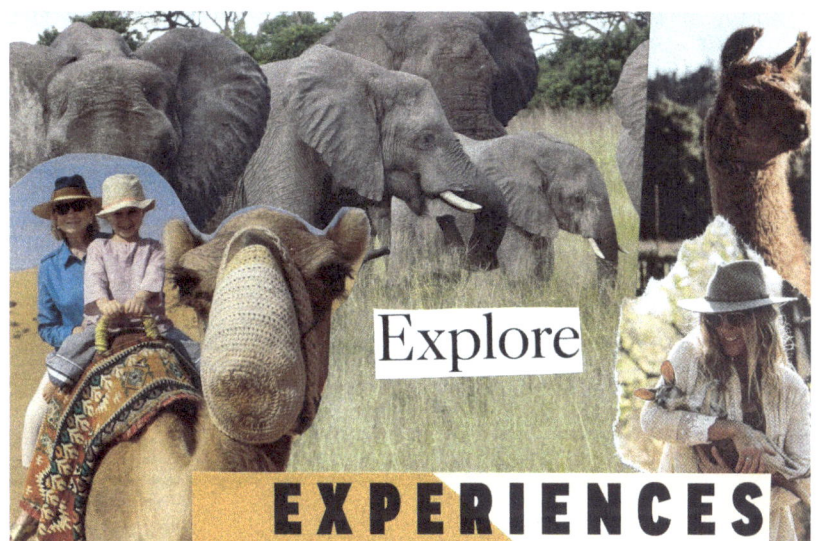

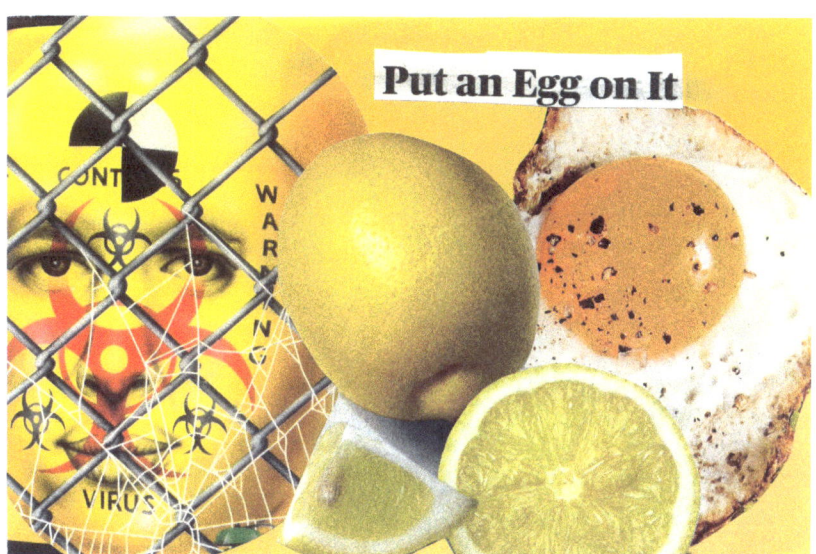

Mary Pendergrass
New Brighton, Minnesota

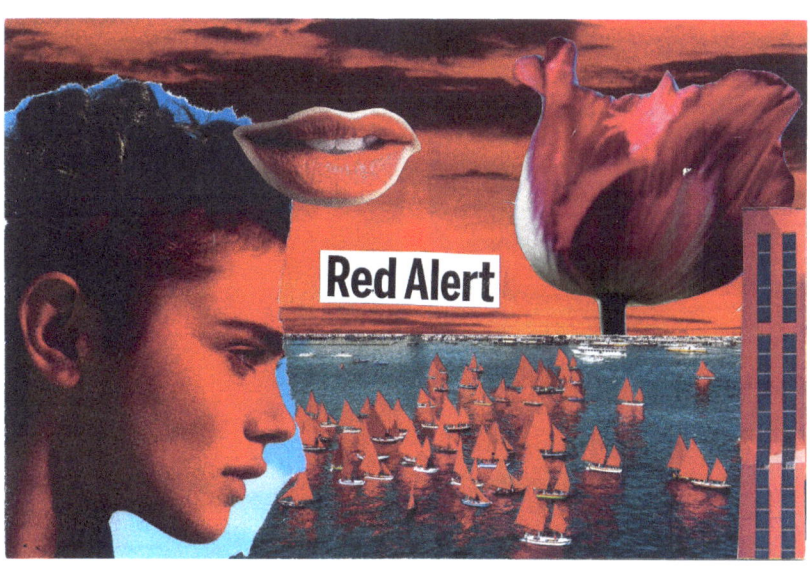

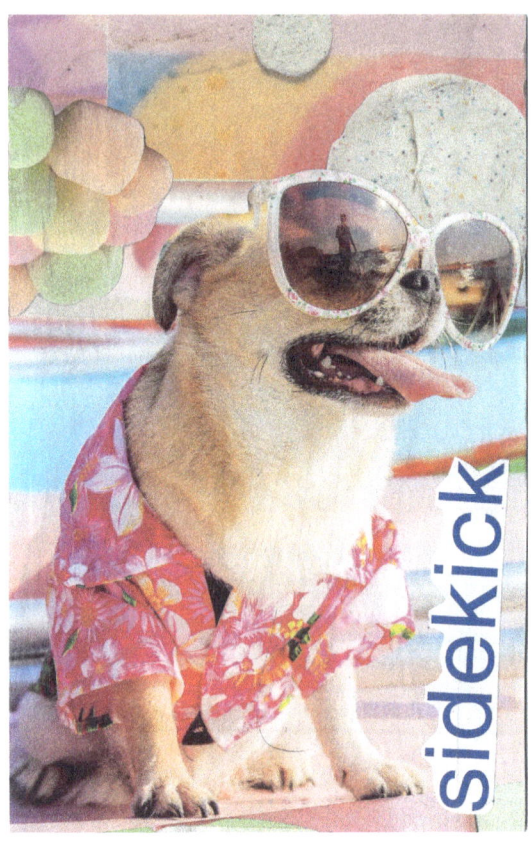

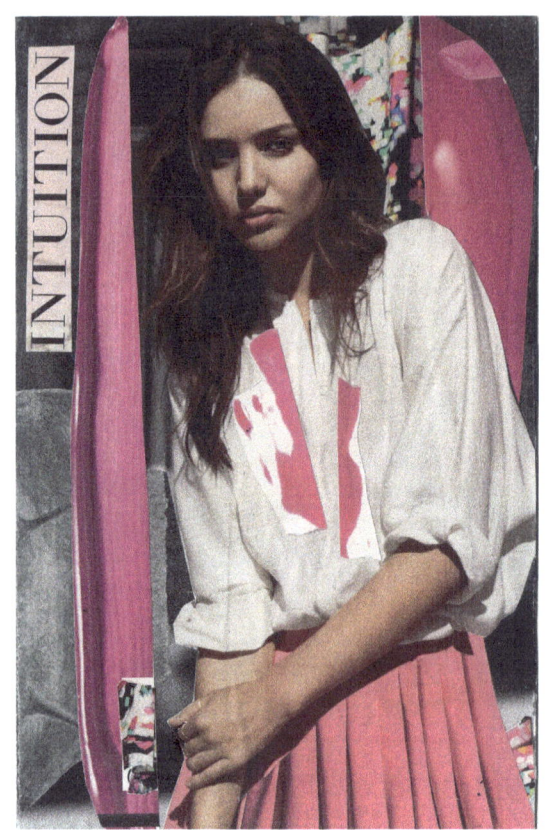

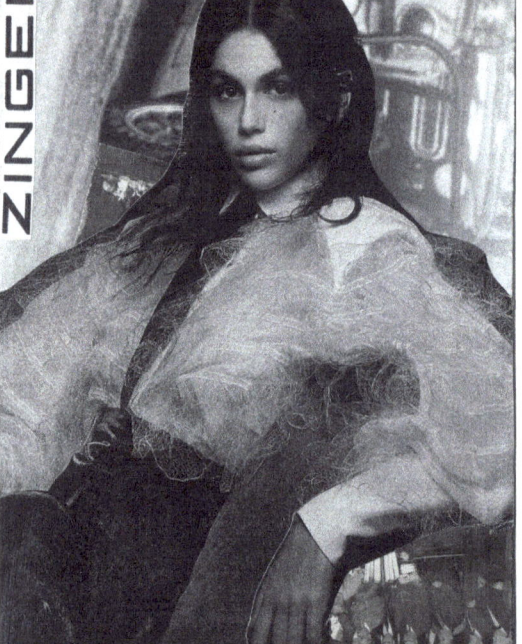

Margaret Richardson
Olympia, Washington

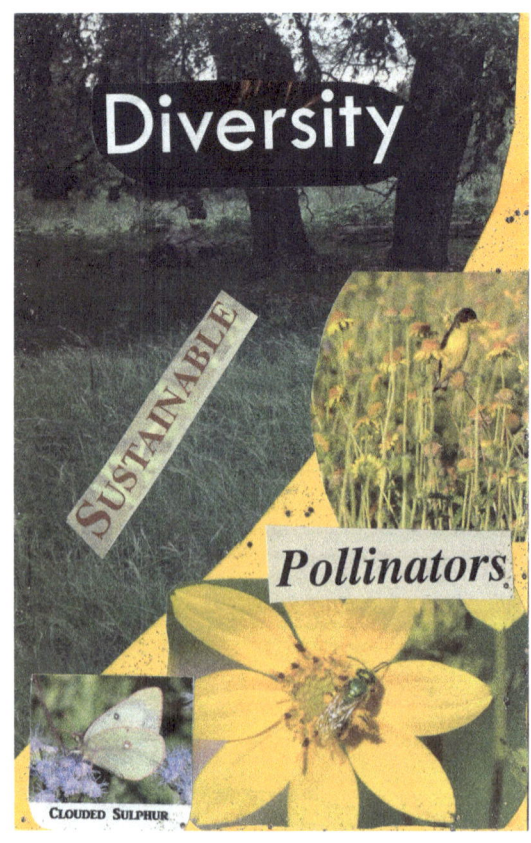

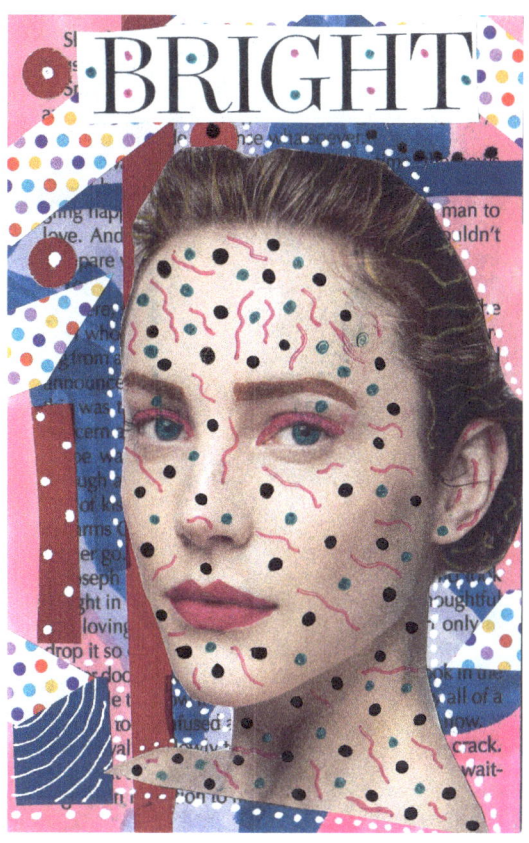

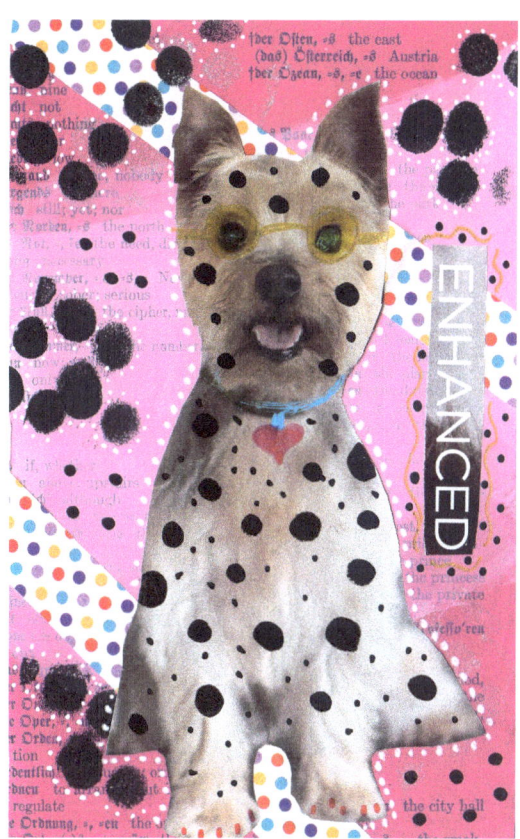

Saundra Burleson
Mesquite, Texas

Amy Jo Garner
Del City, Oklahoma

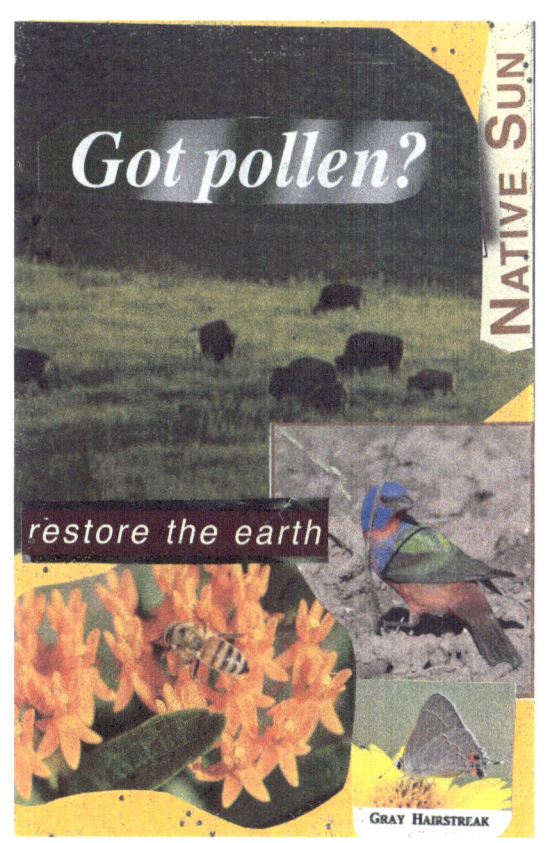

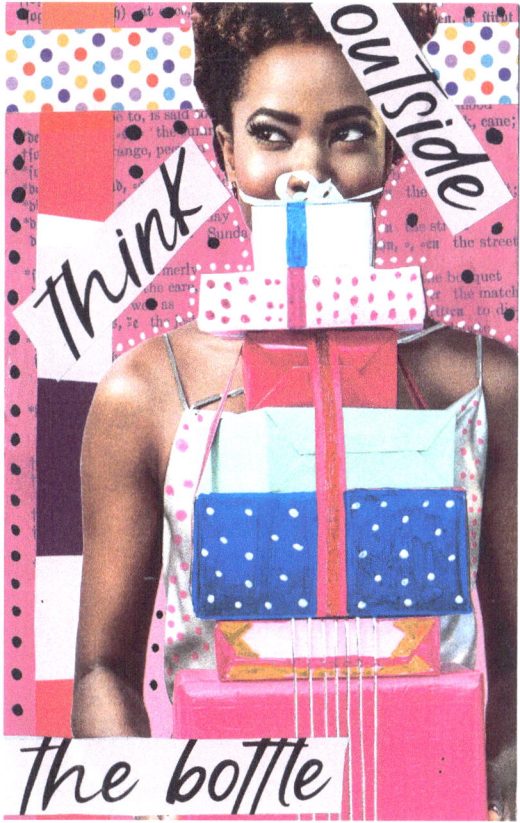

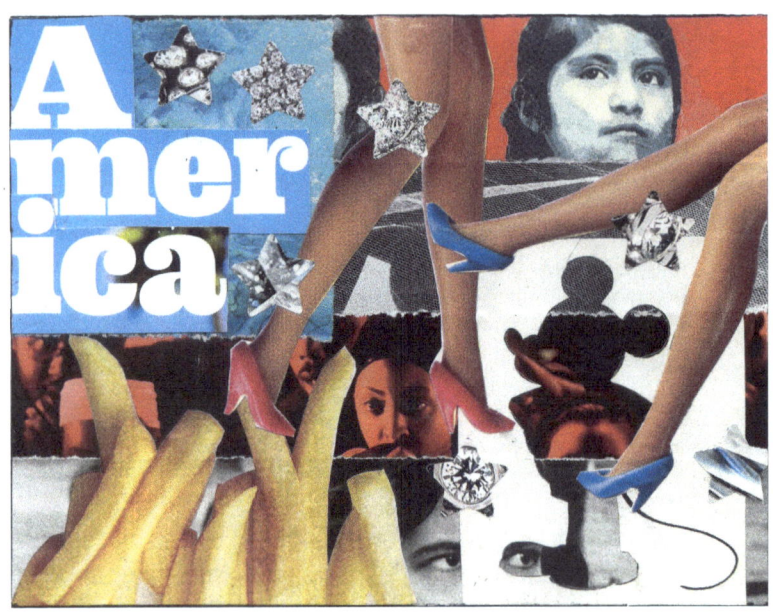

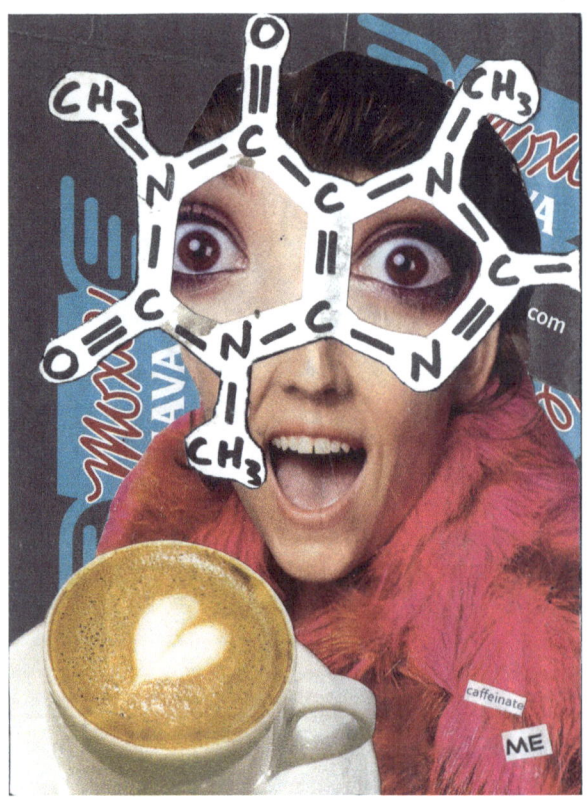

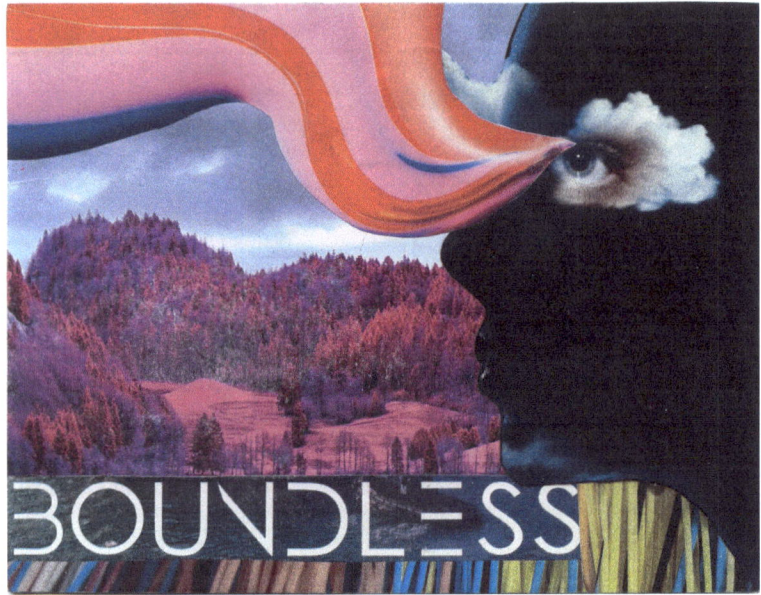

Amy O'Brien
Los Angeles, California

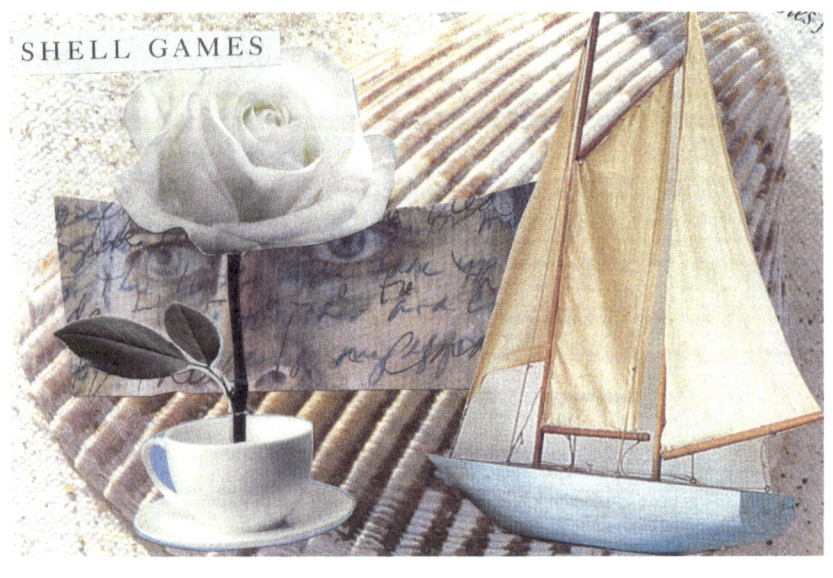

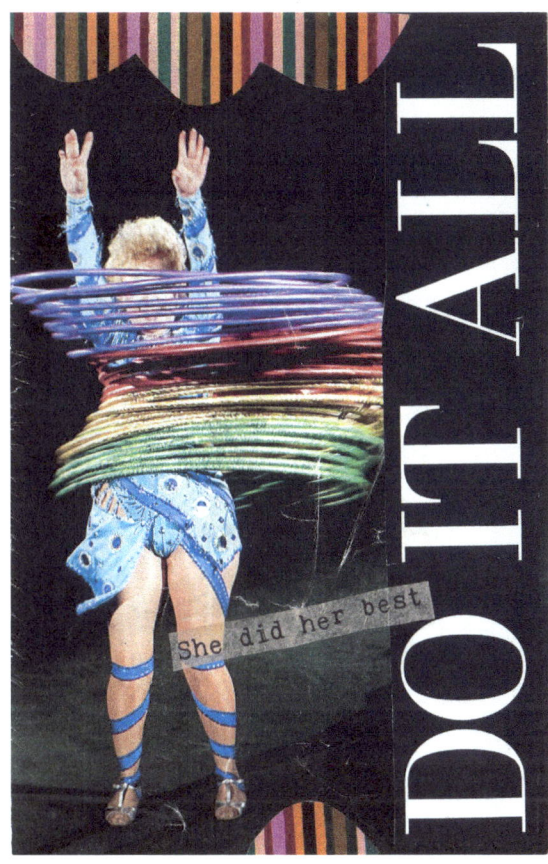

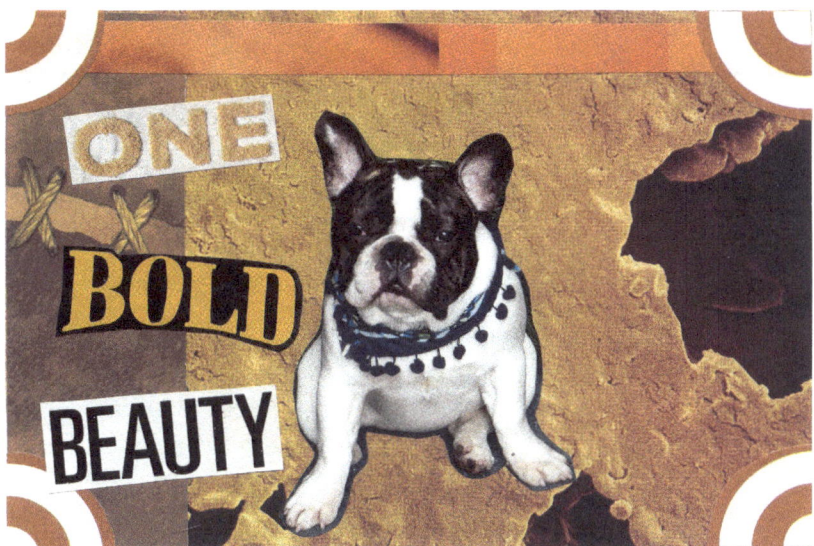

Valerie Orner
Red Bluff, California

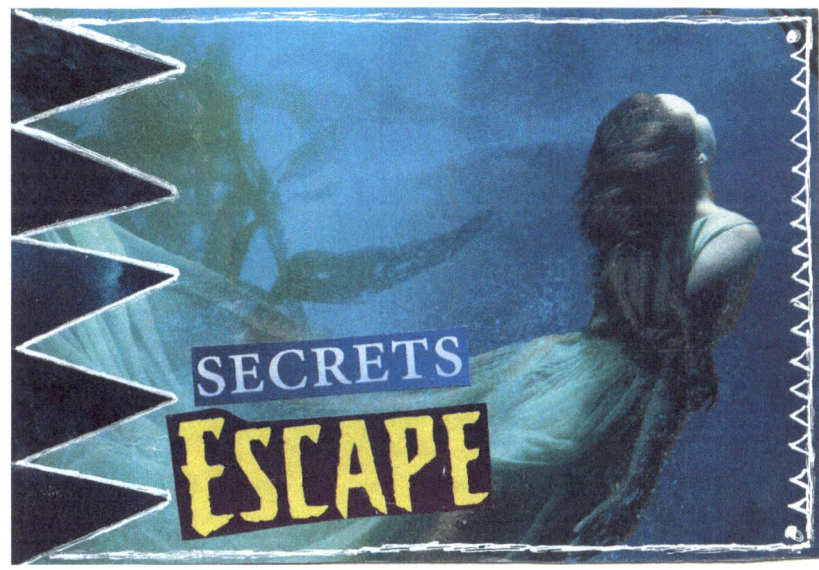

Susan Wilkin
Oklahoma City, Oklahoma

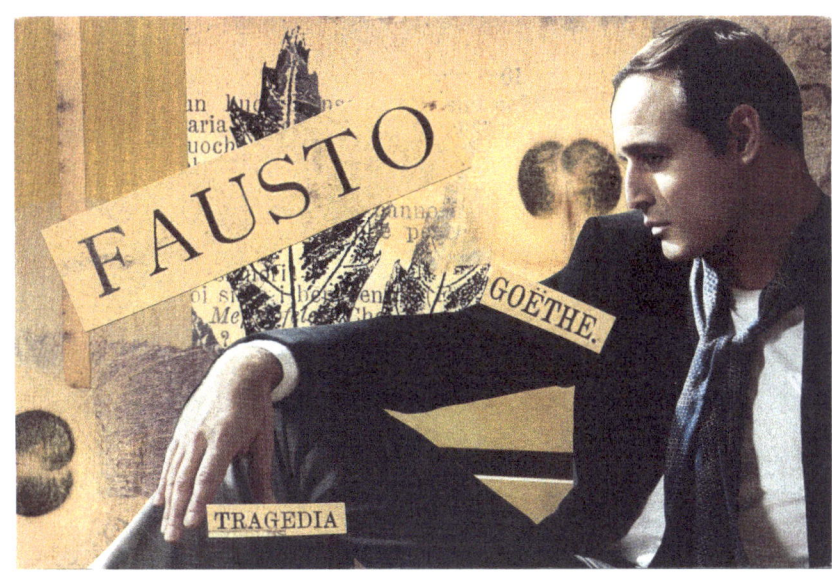

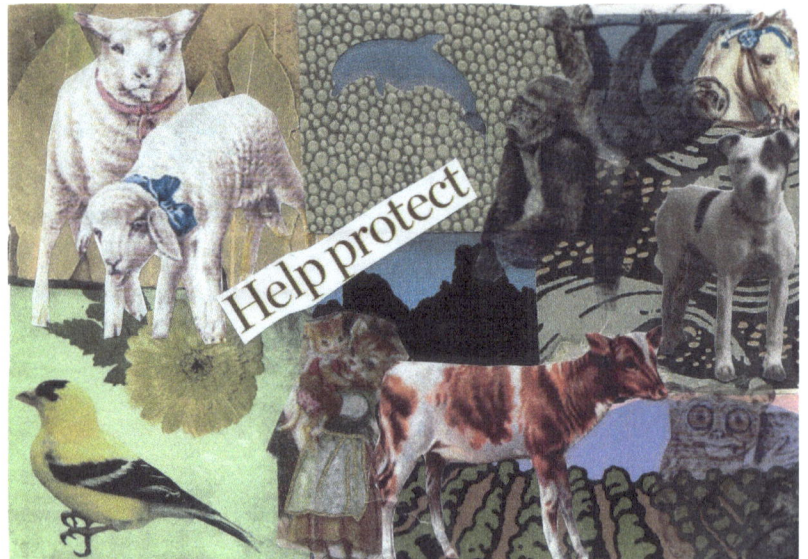

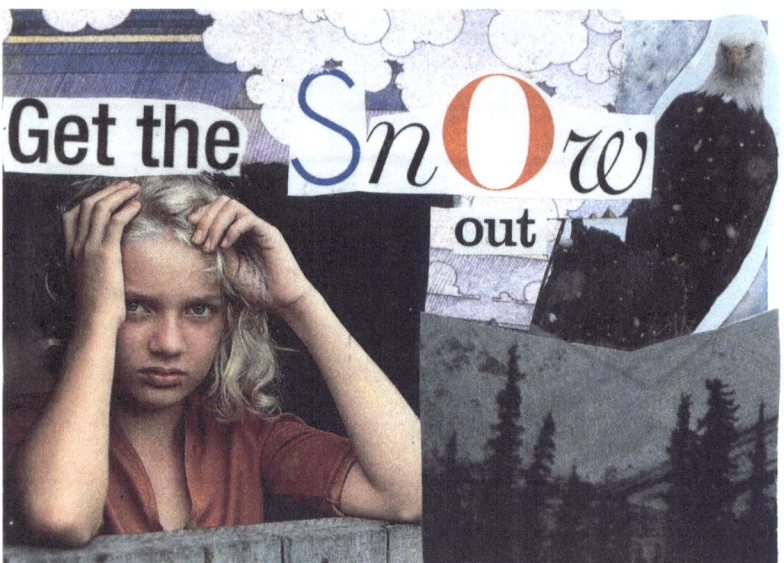

Leslie Trippy
Truckee, California

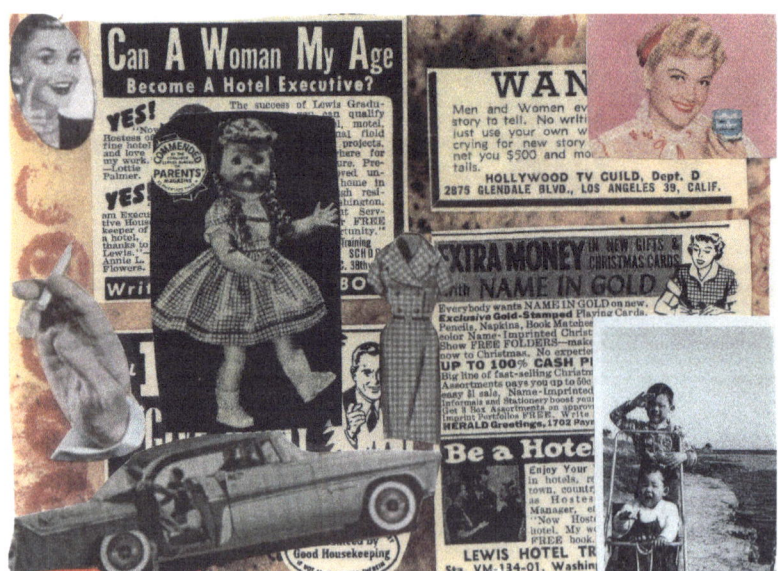

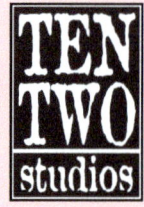